Not Even One

Delores Chapman Danley

WESTBOW
PRESS®
A DIVISION OF THOMAS NELSON
& ZONDERVAN

WestBow Press books may be ordered through booksellers or by contacting:

WestBow Press
A Division of Thomas Nelson & Zondervan
1663 Liberty Drive
Bloomington, IN 47403
www.westbowpress.com
1 (866) 928-1240

Scripture quotations are taken from The Holy Bible, New International Version®, NIV® Copyright © 1973, 1978, 1984, 2011 by Biblica, Inc.® Used by permission. All rights reserved worldwide.

ISBN: 978-1-9736-5730-9 (sc)
ISBN: 978-1-9736-5731-6 (hc)
ISBN: 978-1-9736-5729-3 (e)

Library of Congress Control Number: 2019903179

Print information available on the last page.

WestBow Press rev. date: 03/27/2019

Table of Contents

Introduction

In June of 2011, a book of poetry and devotionals called ***I Think I Heard A Rooster Crow*** first came from a printing press. It contained work that took nine years to write and many life experiences that were sometimes pleasant and sometimes far from pleasant. At that time, I thought that was all that God wanted me to do as far as my writing and publishing adventure was concerned. It didn't take very long for me to discover that the words kept coming, but I had no idea that another book was in the works. I can write poetry only when I am inspired by the Holy Spirit, so the words do not come quickly.

Here I am eight years later, and God has helped me complete a second volume. I had originally planned to title this book ***One Breath Away***, but God had other plans. One day as I sat reading my Bible in my rocking chair on our front porch, I came across **Romans 3:10-12** which states: ***As it is written: "There is no one righteous, not even one; there is no one who understands; there is no one who seeks God. All have turned away, they have together become worthless; there is no one who does good, not even one."*** (NIV) I can't exactly explain it, but His Spirit let me know that the title was to be **Not Even One**. The poem was then sent to my heart along with the idea for the front cover of the book.

That occurred nearly two years before the publication of this book. It is hard to know when a book such as this is finished because there is no storyline with a happily-ever-after ending. However, there are signs and senses that indicate when it is time to put it together and send it to the printing press. Since this is a self-published book, my husband and I thank God for providing the financial means to complete this project. As far as the contents of the book are concerned, all glory also goes only to Him. It is my constant prayer that every word in this book fulfills the plea in **Psalm 19:14---*"May the words of my mouth and the meditation of my heart be pleasing in your sight, O LORD, my Rock and my Redeemer."***

Make Sure
They Know

1 John 5:11-12
And this is the testimony: God has given
us eternal life, and this life is in his Son.
Whoever has the Son has life; whoever does
not have the Son of God does not have life.

He said to them,
"Go into all the world and preach
the gospel to all creation.
Whoever believes and is baptized
will be saved, but whoever does not
believe will be condemned."
Mark 16:15-16 (NIV)

1 Timothy 2:5-6
For there is one God and one mediator between
God and mankind, the man Christ Jesus, who
gave himself as a ransom for all people.

Not Even One

Some people think that living right is all they need to do.
They think that their good deeds and charm will somehow get
them through;
But God has told us differently within His Holy Book.
It's plainly spelled out for us all if we'll just stop and look.
No matter how much good we do we cannot do enough;
But finding God's salvation plan is really not that tough.
The road to Heaven is not built with turns and twists and curves;
It's built on mercy, paved with grace, that none of us deserves.
The Bible clearly tells us that through faith in Christ we're saved,
And the road to our salvation with His blood has been paved.
He is the way, the truth, the life...the straight and narrow path.
Our Father gave His only Son to save us from sin's wrath.
So, if you have not met our Lord, please get to know God's Son;
For not one of us is worthy...oh, no, not even one.

* *

Romans 3:10-12
As it is written: "There is no one righteous, not even one;
there is no one who understands; there is no one who seeks
God. All have turned away, they have together become
worthless; there is no one who does good, not even one."

John 3:16
For God so loved the world that he gave his one and only Son, that
whoever believes in him shall not perish but have eternal life.

John 14:6
Jesus answered, "I am the way and the truth and the life.
No one comes to the Father except through me."

Acts 4:12
Salvation is found in no one else, for there is no other name
under heaven given to men by which we must be saved.

Isaiah 53:6
We all, like sheep, have gone astray, each of us has turned to his
own way; and the LORD has laid on him the iniquity of us all.

* *

One Breath Away

"I always thought I'd have more time," I've heard so many say.
"I would surely have much longer than only yesterday."
We never want to think about how life could end today;
But time here is temporary, and just one breath away.

We may put off 'til tomorrow some debts we should repay.
We may pass a chance to witness to one who's gone astray.
We may wait to ask forgiveness, and think it's all okay;
But our chances may be fleeting, and just one breath away.

We may forget a promise made when we said we would pray.
We may not have fulfilled our vows when God said to obey.
We may have chosen to ignore someone filled with dismay;
But that chance may not come again; it's just one breath away.

It's easy to forget sometimes that we won't always stay,
Because our bodies in this world are only made of clay.
We must prepare with urgency, and we must not delay;
For the time we move to Heaven is just one breath away.

* *

James 4:14
Why, you do not even know what will happen tomorrow.
What is your life? You are a mist that appears
for a little while and then vanishes.

* *

How Good Is Good Enough?

I worked so hard to do my best...
No time for play; no time for rest.
My time was all consumed by "stuff."
I asked, "How good is good enough?"

I never seemed to reach my goal;
I could not win to save my soul.
I wondered as the road got rough,
"Oh, Lord, how good is good enough?"

God let me struggle for a while,
And then He said, "Hear me, my child,
There is no way to reach your goal.
Nothing you do can save your soul.

The works you do must honor me,
For I alone can set you free.
Though you are tough and huff and puff,
Your good is never good enough."

* *

Ephesians 2:8-9
For it is by grace you have been saved, through faith-
--and this not from yourselves, it is the gift of God-
--not by works, so that no one can boast.

* *

The Last Things on His Mind

As Jesus contemplated what He knew lay in store,
His mind was filled with anguish...How could He take much more?
The Romans came to take Him, and He knew all along
That He would be arrested as Judas led the throng.
When He was stripped and beaten, and blood from Him did pour,
I wonder what His thoughts were as He knelt on that floor?
He had so much to ponder, as Peter soon denied
That he ever knew the Christ who once stood by his side.
He stumbled up Calvary amid the taunts and jeers.
What He did for all mankind should bring us all to tears.
Christ bled and died so we can leave all our sins behind.
As He breathed His last, we were the last things on His mind.

* *

John 14:27
Peace I leave with you; my peace I give you. I do not give to you as the
world gives. Do not let your hearts be troubled and do not be afraid.

* *

Grace Lives

When I am asked just how I know
That Jesus saved my soul,
I tell them that long years ago
He came to pay my toll
For all the sins I've ever done
And those I've yet to do.
Now in His eyes my sins are none.
He'll do the same for you.

Because He's done so much for me,
I never could deny
That with His blood He set me free
Although He had to die.
When life tries to tear me apart,
He always brings me through.
He came to dwell within my heart.
He'll do the same for you.

He died and then He rose to live
For all eternity.
What you have done, He will forgive
Just as He did for me.

* *

Romans 6:14
For sin shall no longer be your master, because
you are not under the law but under grace.

* *

By His Scars

How will you know Him when you meet?
Just take a look down at His feet;
And if you still don't understand,
Just ask Him to stretch out His hand.
Then if you still just can't decide,
Reach out and touch His wounded side;
And on His brow is even more
Proof of the crown of thorns He wore.
Another thing you'll recognize
Is all the love seen in His eyes.
Here on Earth or beyond the stars,
You'll recognize Him by His scars.

* *

1 Peter 2:24-25
*"He himself bore our sins" in his body on the cross, so that we
might die to sins and live for righteousness; "by his wounds you
have been healed." For "you were like sheep going astray," but now
you have returned to the Shepherd and Overseer of your souls.*

* *

Just Try

When you meet someone who does not know
How salvation came to earth,
How God sent His Son to us below
And about the virgin birth,
Do you start to sweat and look away
As you think up some way out
And choose to wait for another day
To share what it's all about?
Do you fear you can't find words to say
To tell what Christ means to you?
Just go on and tell it anyway;
God will do what you can't do.
For you may not have another chance
To witness to that lost soul,
And as you utter all your "I can'ts"
He might hear his death bell toll.
Though Satan makes you afraid and shy,
Go on out and testify.
Do not let that chance just pass you by.
Though they may say "No," just try!

* *

Isaiah 52:7
*How beautiful on the mountains are the feet of those who bring
good news, who proclaim peace, who bring good tidings, who
proclaim salvation, who say to Zion, "Your God reigns!"*

* *

He Still Calls Me "Friend"

Judas is a name
    that makes me think "betray."
I read that he came
    to help lead Christ away.
I am quick to judge
    the extent of his greed,
And I might begrudge
    forgiveness for his deed.
Sometimes I forget
    that my guilt is the same,
And I owe a debt
    for all my sin and shame.
At times I neglect
    to put Him first in line,
And then I expect
    some blessings to be mine.
Yes, Judas betrayed,
    but I have often sinned.
Though I too have strayed,
    Jesus still calls me "friend."

* *

Matthew 26:47-50
While he was still speaking, Judas, one of the Twelve, arrived.
With him was a large crowd armed with swords and clubs,
sent from the chief priests and the elders of the people.
Now the betrayer had arranged a signal with them:
"The one I kiss is the man; arrest him."
Going at once to Jesus, Judas said, "Greetings, Rabbi!" and kissed him.
Jesus replied, "Friend, do what you came for."

* *

Hide and Seek

Wouldn't it be wonderful
    if we could hide our shame---
Disguising things we have done
    instead of taking blame?
It seems only natural
    for mankind to deny
The sinful things we have done
    like steal and kill and lie.
Though some consider their faults
    not as bad as others,
No one should cast a stone at
    our sisters and brothers.
God says that we all have sinned
    and often fallen short,
Then desperately turn to Him
    just as a last resort.
We must remember God knows
    what we try to suppress.
It's futile to run and hide;
    we might as well confess.

* *

Psalm 90:8
You have set our iniquities before you, our secret
sins in the light of your presence.

* *

Homeless

"Mama, what does 'homeless' mean?" the little boy inquired.
She said, "You have no place to go when you're sick and tired.
It means you're lost in this world with no place of your own;
And often life seems hopeless, and you feel all alone.
By some you are rejected; some think you have no worth;
And you might start to question why God put you on earth.
But, Son, our Lord and Savior was often homeless, too.
He came here on a mission and was just passing through.
Now we, like Christ, often feel this world's so full of sin
That it cannot be the home we were meant to live in.
So, Son, we must remember that we are homeless, too.
One day we'll be rejoicing when home comes into view."

* *

John 14:2-3
My Father's house has many rooms; if that were not so, would I
have told you that I am going there to prepare a place for you?
And if I go and prepare a place for you, I will come back and
take you to be with me that you also may be where I am.

* *

Looking for a Smile

I went out looking for a smile today
In many busy places,
But all I discovered along the way
Were many frowning faces.
I saw some people so full of sadness
They struggled to hide their tears.
A few appeared on the edge of madness
And could not disguise their fears.
As I kept searching for a friendly face,
I was starting to despair.
Though I met many of the human race,
I saw no smile anywhere.
I wondered why it was such a hard chore
Just to find a happy grin.
I knew we could use miles of smiles galore
In this world so filled with sin.
Then, all at once, a thought came to my mind
When I saw my reflection.
All the wear and tear of my daily grind
Filled my face with dejection.
How could I hope to discover a smile
From some strangers that I met
When they may have been seeking all the while
What I had not given yet?

* *

Psalm 68:3
But may the righteous be glad and rejoice before God;
May they be happy and joyful.

* *

He Sees Red

There's an old adage I've often heard said
When someone is angry, "He really sees red."
A bull gets so mad and lowers his head
When a bullfighter waves a cape crimson red.
God filled Pharaoh's heart with anger and dread
When Egypt's firstborn were found to be dead.
Then all Pharaoh's men found they were misled
And drowned in a sea so aptly named Red.

But God saved his own by blood that was shed
And led them safely through deserts ahead.
Centuries later Christ stood in our stead;
He died for our sins and suffered and bled.
From that flowing blood, the Evil One fled
As all of our sins were covered in red.
Red once meant anger, but now love instead.
When God looks at me, I pray He sees red.

* *

1 John 1:7
But if we walk in the light, as he is in the light, we
have fellowship with one another, and the blood
of Jesus, his Son, purifies us from all sin.

Hebrews 9:12
He did not enter by means of the blood of goats and
calves; but he entered the Most Holy Place once for all by
his own blood, having obtained eternal redemption.

Ephesians 1:7-8
In him we have redemption through his blood, the forgiveness
of sins, in accordance with the riches of God's grace that
he lavished on us with all wisdom and understanding.

* *

Ripples

I have skipped many stones across this time I call life;
Some brought me pleasure, but so many brought me strife.
Some stones were called envy, bringing no satisfaction.
Some were called self-pity, with "woe-is-me" reaction.
Some were stones of anger, with ripples never ending;
Those caused much destruction, with fences needing mending.
Hatred stones reached farther than any other kind...
Feelings that I surely do not want to leave behind.
Unforgiveness skipped on the hard surface of my heart...
Each stone a reminder of some friendship torn apart.
Each time that I picked up a destructive stone to throw,
I only hurt myself every time I let one go.
Now that I am older, I pray I will never cast
Another harmful stone that has ripples traveling fast.
There are so many stones so available to me,
Such as love and patience and forgiveness, to name three.
I hope to choose some stones so much better than before,
And pray that their ripples help me land on Heaven's shore.

* *

Ephesians 4:29,31,32

*(v 29) Do not let any unwholesome talk come out of your
mouths, but only what is helpful for building others up according
to their needs, that it may benefit those who listen.*

*(v 31) Get rid of all bitterness, rage and anger, brawling
and slander, along with every form of malice.*

*(v 32) Be kind and compassionate to one another, forgiving
each other, just as in Christ God forgave you.*

* *

The Power of the Promise

There is power in His promise that He will never leave.
He is with us when we're happy and with us when we grieve.
He is here to reassure us when we feel all alone.
He is here to supply us all with strength to carry on.
He is with us in our triumphs and with us when we fail.
He is with us in the church house and with us in the jail.
He is on the field of battle in lands so far away.
He is with us as we labor and with us as we play.
He is with us when we're homeless and with us when we're not.
He is with the rich and famous and those the world forgot.
He is with us while we're living and as we face our death.
He is with us every moment from first to our last breath.
Yes, there's power in His promise, for He can never lie.
He will always be beside us...on that we can rely!

* *

Deuteronomy 31:6
Be strong and courageous. Do not be afraid or terrified
because of them, for the LORD your God goes with
you; he will never leave you nor forsake you.

Romans 4: 20-21
Yet he did not waver through unbelief regarding the promise of
God, but was strengthened in his faith and gave glory to God, being
fully persuaded that God had power to do what he had promised.

* *

The Only World That Matters

I'm living in a world of "in between."
God planned me in my home so far away.
When I made my appearance on this scene,
God never had in mind for me to stay.
I guess from the start, somewhere in my heart,
I've known I was just visiting this place.
When this tour is over, I shall depart
And leave this world behind without a trace.
So much of this life seems to be uphill,
And often I might find it in tatters.
His promises are true, and soon I will
Go home to the only world that matters.

* *

John 14:1-4

"Do not let your hearts be troubled. Trust in God; trust also in me. In my Father's house are many rooms; if it were not so, I would have told you. I am going there to prepare a place for you. And if I go and prepare a place for you, I will come back and take you to be with me that you also may be where I am. You know the way to the place where I am going."

* *

NAMES

I used to have a memory as sharp as a tack.
If I read something just one time, I could quote it back.
Now as I've chalked up many years, life is playing games.
It seems that for the life of me I can't recall names.

When thinking of one I know well, my mind plays some tricks.
Then I go through the alphabet hoping something clicks.
Though age has dimmed my memory, I need never fret;
My name is written in a book God will not forget.

* *

Revelation 21:27
Nothing impure will ever enter it, nor will anyone who
does what is shameful or deceitful, but only those whose
names are written in the Lamb's book of life.

* *

Joy

I've made up my mind to be joyful today.
Yes, that is the choice I have made.
I don't really know just what might come my way;
It could be some sunshine or shade.
I did not say "happy" or "gleeful," you see,
For that's not the same as "joy."
Happiness changes as life happens to me,
And some things in life just annoy.
So, whether I'm happy, or whether I'm sad,
There still will be joy I can find.
There's always a little of good with the bad.
I choose joy! I've made up my mind!

* *

John 15:11
*I have told you this so that my joy may be in you
and that your joy may be complete.*

Romans 15:13
*May the God of hope fill you with all joy and peace
as you trust in him, so that you may overflow
with hope by the power of the Holy Spirit.*

* *

Micah 6:8
And what does the LORD require of you?
To act justly and to love mercy and to
walk humbly with your God.

Jesus Walked the Back Roads

I love to walk the back roads where life slows down its pace,
And I commune with nature far from this world's rat race.
My Jesus often traveled far off the beaten path
As He talked to his Father without turmoil or wrath.
The hustle and the bustle in this old world today
Provides me with a longing to find a hideaway.
For I must find a haven where I feel the Spirit;
A place of peace and quiet so my soul can hear it.
So, for some precious hours, we walk, my Lord and I;
We talk and laugh together, and sometimes we just cry.
What joy it is to travel the back roads of my life
And just talk to my Savior away from toil and strife.

* *

Mark 16:12
*Afterward Jesus appeared in a different form to two
of them while they were walking in the country.*

Luke 6:12
*One of those days Jesus went out to a mountainside
to pray, and spent the night praying to God.*

* *

God Is Love

Proverbs 3:3
Let love and faithfulness never leave
you; bind them around your neck, write
them on the tablet of your heart.

The Greatest of These

"What do you want me to do?" I would ask
My Savior from time-to-time.
"Is there some specific, difficult task,
Or some mountain I should climb?
Should I sell all I own and give away
My treasures here on this earth
To help some lost soul who has gone astray?
How much is a lost soul worth?
Do you want me to visit those in jail
Or help those with addictions?
So many people are not doing well
Suffering from afflictions.
Many have never heard the great story
How You can save them from sin.
Shall I go forth and speak of your glory
And how through You they can win?
Christ, what should I do for my King of Kings
To serve your kingdom above?"
"My child," He said, "just do all of these things,
But it must begin with love."

* *

1 Corinthians 13:13
And now these three remain: faith, hope and
love. But the greatest of these is love.

* *

The Second Greatest Commandment

We may sit in a building called "church" all we please.
We may even say all of our prayers on our knees;
But if we have no compassion for God's "least of these,"
Then the second commandment is lost in a breeze.

For He says to love God above any other,
But the second in line is love for our brother.
For Jesus said that we must love one another,
And that includes more than our father and mother.

Many people have traveled wrong roads that they chose,
So, others may think they are much better than those;
But God's Word is recorded so everyone knows
That we are saved by the blood of Sharon's Sweet Rose.

An outer appearance may be all that we see
When we look at each other, but that shouldn't be.
We must open our hearts, and Christ's love is the key;
For our God sees no difference between you and me.

* *

Mark 12:30-31
"Love the Lord your God with all your heart and with all
your soul and with all you mind and with all your strength.
The second is this: 'Love your neighbor as yourself.'
There is no commandment greater than these."

* *

Love Never Fails

I thought I'd test a concept my Bible says is true,
So, I decided I would just see what I could do
To either prove or disprove that love will never fail.
I started in the places I'd always known so well.
Though someone hurt me deeply, I chose to let it go.
I offered sweet forgiveness, and love began to grow.
From anger and hard feelings, a friendship did prevail
That was one step to prove that real love will never fail.
I shared God's love with beggars I met out on the street
By giving them some warm smiles and sometimes food to eat.
Their gratitude amazed me, for little had I done;
But love will never fail you when shared with God's own Son.
I showed God's love to addicts who struggled with despair
And many with afflictions, for they were everywhere.
I visited with shut-ins and those locked up in jails,
And each time I could see that our God's love never fails.
It's easy to show love to our family and friends,
But those who least deserve it must be where love extends.
For we are in that number who sin in great detail,
And we must count our blessings that God's love will not fail.
Romantic love is precious, and we all hope to find
A love that's strong and faithful and the forever kind;
But we're to love all people along life's rocky trails,
And God gives us his promise that real love never fails.

* *

John 15:17
This is my command: Love each other.

* *

If I Don't Love

If I don't love beggars on the street,
    Am I like Christ?
If I don't love those filled with deceit,
    Am I like Christ?
If I don't love the cheat and the thief,
    Am I like Christ?
If I don't love all those filled with grief,
    Am I like Christ?
If I don't love people who annoy,
    Am I like Christ?
If I don't love the ones who destroy,
    Am I like Christ?
If I don't love those hateful and mean,
    Am I like Christ?
If I don't love those vile and obscene,
    Am I like Christ?
If I don't love those hurting me so,
    Am I like Christ?
If I don't love all those here below,
    Am I like Christ?
Since God is Love, that's all He can do.
That's what He asks of me and of you.

* *

1 Corinthians 13:1-3
*If I speak in the tongues of men or of angels, but do not have love,
I am only a resounding gong or a clanging cymbal. If I have the gift
of prophecy and can fathom all mysteries and all knowledge, and if
I have a faith that can move mountains, but do not have love, I am
nothing. If I give all I possess to the poor and give over my body to
hardship that I may boast, but do not have love, I gain nothing.*

* *

Will You Still Love Me?

Lord, when I fail you again,
  Will you still love me?
Lord, when I give in to sin,
  Will you still love me?
Lord, when I stumble and fall,
  Will you still love me?
Lord, when I've wasted it all,
  Will you still love me?

  Yes, Child, I will still love you.

Child, when you don't get your way,
  Will you still love me?
Child, when skies turn to gray,
  Will you still love me?
Child, when I ask you to wait,
  Will you still love me?
Child, when you think I am late,
  Will you still love me?

  Yes, Lord, I will still love you.

* *

Psalm 63:3-4
Because your love is better than life, my lips will glorify you.
I will praise you as long as I live, and in
your name I will lift up my hands.

* *

Why I Love You Best

Wade, I love you best because you are our first child and only son. I love your kind heart and generosity. I love your forgiving nature. I love your sense of humor and your honesty. I love the way you make friends everywhere you go. I love you for always being a "Mama's boy." I love how hardworking you are. I love you because, in a way, we grew up together. Yes, I love you best.

Stacey, I love you best because you are our only daughter. I love your sense of style. I love your carefree spirit. I love the way you can take life head-on with absolutely no fear. I love your independence. I love your beauty, both inside and out...but especially from the inside. I love the fact that you are a teacher, just as I once was, and I love the way you love your students. I love your compassion for other people and helpless animals. Yes, I love you best.

Britt, I love you best because you are our first grandchild and oldest grandson. I love you because you are an "overcomer" who can surmount all obstacles in your way. I love you for your sense of pride and for your ability to always stand your ground. I love how you take care of your family. I love the fact that you have ambition and work hard to accomplish your dreams. I love the man you have become. Yes, I love you best.

Gage, I love you best because you are our second grandson. I love you because of your tender heart and concern for others. I love you for the way you enjoy life and for your loyalty to your family and friends. I love you because you are always willing to help anyone who needs it. I love you because you always let me rock you when you were little because you said that I was soft and comfortable. I love you because you think that I am the greatest cook in the world. I love your hugs. Yes, I love you best.

Tanner, I love you best because you are our third grandson and such a big part of our lives. I love you for always standing up for yourself. I love you for being a survivor throughout all of your trials. I love you for striving to be the man you really want to be. I love you for the love you have for children and for your family. I love you because you have taught us many lessons in life that were not always easy but were necessary for us to grow in our faith. I love you for never giving up and for being our prodigal son who finally came home. Yes, I love you best.

Gracie, I love you best because you are our only granddaughter. I love your sweet nature but also for the fact that you will stand up for yourself when necessary. I love your compassion with elderly people and helpless animals. I love your smile and beautiful golden hair. I love how talented and intelligent you are, but I would still love you the same even if you weren't. Yes, I love you best.

Ford, I love you best because you are our fourth grandson and our last grandchild---our baby. I love you for the ultimate joy you have brought to our family. I love your adventurous nature and your fearlessness. I love how loving and affectionate you are and the warm hugs you willingly share with everyone. I love the way you never seem to meet a stranger and how you accept everyone just as they are. I love your honesty with "no holds barred." Yes, I love you best.

Mike, I love you the very best because, without you, I would not have all of these others to love. I love you for the tenderness that you are not ashamed to show to the world. I love you for your generous nature. I love you for all that you do for me and for our family. I love you for your subtle sense of humor. I love the way we can communicate without speaking. I love how we often say the same thing at the same time. I love you for always telling me that you have fun just sharing experiences with me, no matter what we are doing. I love you for overlooking my faults. I love you for the man you are. Yes, I love you the very best.

Where Love Lives

My parents brought me up to know
That there's a God who's real.
By their example they would show
They weren't afraid to kneel.
I wonder if, had they not been
The ones who led the way,
Would I be lost in all my sin
Instead of saved today?
What if there had not been someone
To make sure that I heard
About our God and all He's done
And introduced His Word?
I wonder if those who receive
A witness up in age
Find it much harder to believe
As they read page by page?
Some say His Word's a fairy tale
And it cannot be true,
But I can speak in great detail
Of things He's helped me through.
It's hard for me to realize
That some just won't accept
The evidence before their eyes
And hearts where love is kept.
They think we're foolish and naïve
To trust in things unseen.
They'd rather laugh at us or grieve
Or something in between.

I know they feel that there's much more
Than life on earth and death,
And don't they wonder what's in store
When they take their last breath?
A bitter heart, though it resists,

Has some love dwelling there.
Love never dies once it exists,
And love must live somewhere.
So, people who say they abstain
From thinking life goes on,
Should tell me how they can explain
Where all the love has gone.

* *

Psalm 23:6
*Surely goodness and love will follow me all the days of my
life, and I will dwell in the house of the LORD forever.*

* *

East to West

Someone hurt me badly and left a scar so deep,
I reacted, sadly, with words I could not keep.
I spread the word around of hateful things she'd said;
And every chance I found, I almost wished her dead!
How dare she say such things about one such as I?
Words such as hers are stings and cause my eyes to cry.
Forgiveness was a word I wanted to ignore,
For it would be absurd to love her like before.
Why should I be the one to lend a hand of grace?
Why, after all she's done, I'd like to slap her face!
How can I be so kind when she made such a slur?
Why should I bring to mind just what good friends we were?
Then Jesus butted in as thoughts ran through my head,
Reminding me of sin and hurtful things I've said.
He told me how I've failed the One who died for me,
And how His hands were nailed to Calvary's cruel tree.
Forgiveness was approved from Him who loves us best.
My sins have been removed as far as east to west.
Forgiveness does not end, now I can plainly see;
I must forgive my friend as Jesus forgave me.

* *

Psalm 103:11-12
*For as high as the heavens are above the earth, so great is
his love for those who fear him; as far as the east is from the
west, so far has he removed our transgressions from us.*

* *

God Made
A Way

Psalm 27:5
For in the day of trouble he will keep
me safe in his dwelling; he will hide
me in the shelter of his sacred tent
and set me high upon a rock.

God Made a Way

God made a way,
Though no end was in sight.
God made a way,
Through one more long, dark night.
God made a way
And turned the wrong to right.
God made a way
When we lost strength to fight.
God made a way,
Though hopeless seemed our plight.
God made a way,
For wondrous is His might.
God made a way,
Now everything's alright.
God made a way.

* *

Isaiah 43:16-21
This is what the LORD says---he who made a way through the
sea, a path through the mighty waters, who drew out the chariots
and horses, the army and reinforcements together, and they lay
there, never to rise again, extinguished, snuffed out like a wick:
"Forget the former things; do not dwell on the past. See, I am
doing a new thing! Now it springs up; do you not perceive it? I am
making a way in the wilderness and streams in the wasteland."

* *

Hardships

Looking down a long, dark tunnel through problems that we faced,
The life we knew just slipped away and could not be replaced.
There seemed to be no earthly way to meet obligations.
Our spirits had grown weary of trials and tribulations.
Sometimes I prayed for God to come and carry me away,
But He thought I should stay right here and fight another day.
When troubles come so late in life, we wonder how we can
Find stamina to overcome as when we first began.
But God tells us He often used people of all ages.
The Bible gives examples of that throughout its pages.
Yes, God assigned important tasks to people "up in years,"
And when they felt incapable, He helped them face their fears.
So God reminded me of men like Abraham and Paul
And His faithful servant Moses who struggled through it all.
Yes, all the hardships that we face can make us weak or strong.
It is our choice to just give up or try to right the wrong.
We need to think of challenges as pathways to explore;
For when we see no earthly way, God opens a new door.

* *

2 Timothy 4:5
But you, keep your head in all situations, endure hardship, do the
work of an evangelist, discharge all the duties of your ministry.

* *

Broken

Yes, I have been broken, haven't you?
Time and time again I've tried to fix
Wounds caused by myself or someone who
Threw some hurtful stones and cruel sticks.
I try to hide the scars left behind
As I glue piece-by-piece back in place.
Yet, always there's some piece I can't find.
Still I keep patching on..."just in case."
No matter how I try to control
All the reconstruction that I need,
I find I cannot make myself whole.
Though I work hard, I just can't succeed.
When all else fails, I pick up my mess
And ask God what I did that was wrong.
He says, "Child, why don't you just confess
You should have trusted me all along?"
For when I let God make each repair
And do the things I myself can't do,
He leaves not one sign of wear and tear,
And I am once again like brand new.

****

2 Corinthians 5:17
*Therefore, if anyone is in Christ, he is a new
creation; the old has gone, the new has come!*

Psalm 51:17
*The sacrifices of God are a broken spirit; a broken
and contrite heart, O God, you will not despise.*

****

Through the Pain

Sometimes I see beauty beyond my window pane.
Sometimes I see sunshine, and sometimes I see rain.
Sometimes birds are singing; sometimes the thunder rolls.
Sometimes a memory takes melancholy strolls.

Sometimes I see heartache as I look through my pain.
Sometimes I see myself all covered with sin's stain.
Sometimes my spirits fall, and I feel so alone.
It's then I remember that God's still on His throne.

* *

Psalm 47:8
God reigns over the nations;
God is seated on his holy throne.

* *

Have I Forgotten?

When I go through trials and nothing goes right
And life hardly seems worthwhile,
I may start to ponder on my sorry plight
And think all the world is vile.
I cannot understand what I could have done
To deserve what I must bear.
Storm clouds gather around and shut out the sun.
Each step I take is a snare.
Self-pity and sorrow take over my mind;
All I seem to do is mope.
Happiness and laughter are all left behind;
I seem to have lost all hope.
Somehow, I've forgotten the good things in life;
I cover my face in shame.
My blessings outnumber my troubles and strife,
I have too many to name.

* *

Deuteronomy 6:11(b)-12
---then when you eat and are satisfied, be careful
that you do not forget the LORD, who brought you
out of Egypt, out of the land of slavery.

* *

The Battle

Broken and bleeding
Hope was receding
My soul was pleading
No more! No more!

Life just kept crashing
My hopes were dashing
Great waves were lashing
On my life's shore.

Darkness was testing
No time for resting
I kept requesting
Blessings to pour.

I was beseeching
Begging and screeching
Prayers were reaching
For Heaven's door.

My God was hearing
Comfort was nearing
Heaven was cheering
The One I adore.

* *

Romans 12:12
Be joyful in hope, patient in affliction, faithful in prayer.

* *

Battle Fatigue

I do get tired of waiting
When sin seems to be winning
When people keep on hating
When people keep on sinning
When people keep on lying
When people keep on cheating
When I am tired from trying
When my strength keeps depleting.
I do get tired of fighting
When it seems I am losing
When people keep backbiting
When loved ones keep refusing
When no one hears my pleading
When life keeps rearranging
When morals are receding
When preachers are shortchanging.
But God says, "Keep on going
And keep your lamplight burning
One day the seeds you're sowing
At last you'll see returning
And even though you're weary
You must keep on believing
I promise you sincerely
Harvests you'll be receiving.

* *

Galatians 6:9
Let us not become weary in doing good, for at the proper
time we will reap a harvest if we do not give up.

* *

But God

I was as low as I could go;
Despair had dragged me down so low.
My happiness had turned to woe,
But God refused to leave me so.

Danger I did not recognize
Was all around before my eyes.
My choices were not very wise,
But God kept me from my demise.

At times I felt some foolish pride
And let it build up deep inside.
Still, I was never satisfied,
But God stepped in and changed the tide.

So many times, while on this sod,
Through many snares my feet have trod.
I could have been in Satan's squad,
But God has been my lightning rod.

My life could end with just one nod,
But God....

* *

Galatians 6:9
Let us not become weary in doing good, for at the proper
time we will reap a harvest if we do not give up.

* *

ME	CHRIST
My wounds are deep;	His wounds were deep;
My will is gone.	His will was done.
How can I hope	Now we have hope
To carry on?	From God's own Son.
My broken heart	His broken heart
Is bruised and sore.	Cried out for man.
I just cannot	What we cannot,
Take anymore.	With God we can.
Now I have scars	Where are the scars?
I just can't hide,	They're in his side,
And my pain is	As on the cross
Not justified.	Our Savior died.
Or maybe I	Scars in his hands
Have caused my pain,	And on his brow,
And through my loss	His blood was spilled
I've much to gain.	To save us now;
For Jesus Christ	And nothing can
Broke down the bars,	Keep us apart.
And now I see	Where are the scars?
The need for scars.	They're in his heart.

* *

Philippians 4:13
I can do all this through him who gives me strength.

* *

Know My Thoughts

Psalm 107:43
Let the one who is wise heed these things
and ponder the loving deeds of the LORD.

Flipped Switches

Shortly after we bought our first house, I was working inside while our son, daughter, and one of their cousins were playing outside. They were young at the time but old enough to play close to the house without constant supervision. (At least that is what I thought at the time.) As I was working, the electricity went off, so I went to check the switch box. The breaker had tripped. I flipped it back on and immediately heard a scream from the carport. The breaker tripped again, cutting off the electric current. I rushed outside to find our daughter holding the raw end of what was left of an old extension cord. The other end was plugged into the receptacle on the carport. Our son and his cousin were laughing because they had talked our daughter into holding the raw end of the cord while they plugged it in. They thought that would be a very funny thing to watch. They did not realize that she could have been electrocuted had the breaker not switched off the current. To this very day it still frightens me to think what might have happened but for the grace of God.

I wonder how many times God comes to our rescue when we do not even realize it? I also think about the times when everything in life seems to go wrong and we think that God is punishing us for some reason we do not understand. Sometimes God "flips the switches" on things we think we want or need because He knows they are not good for us. Looking back over many disappointments throughout my life, I can see---since hindsight is 20/20 vision---that what I wanted would have been a huge mistake. What appeared to be a disappointment turned out to be a blessing. How I thank God for all of those "flipped switches" in my life!

* *

Isaiah 55:8
"For my thoughts are not your thoughts, neither are your ways my ways," declares the Lord.

* *

A Little Bit of All Three

On many occasions I have read the account of the Parable of the Lost Son, also known as the Prodigal Son, in **Luke 15:11-32**. That parable hits very closely to home with me, because we have struggled with prodigals from time to time. I also realize that I have a little bit of a prodigal within my own spirit, because I have often strayed from my Heavenly Father for short periods of time. I have followed my own desires and feelings instead of listening to God my Father. Often, I have had to pay the consequences that always come as a result of being a prodigal. I can identify with that son.

I also know how a parent feels whenever an errant child goes astray. There is a feeling of helplessness, hopelessness, and heartache. There is a longing to see that child and to know that he (or she) is safe. Often, the hardest part is "not knowing." That child is always on my mind, even though life goes on as normally as possible. My ears are always listening for a call, and my eyes are ever alert for a sight of that child. When he comes into view, I am waiting to run out and meet him with open arms...no matter what. Yes, I can identify with that father.

What I have not always realized is that I am sometimes like that older brother who feels left out and unappreciated. This does not pertain to my children who have gone astray, because nothing could ever change my love and forgiveness for them. However, on some otherwise happy occasions involving other people, I have simply refused to "attend the party." Pride and selfishness often get in the way of rejoicing for the good fortune of others, especially if I have been hurt by that person. Jealousy rears its ugly head, and sometimes I let it linger a little too long. I might feel that he does not deserve to be accepted and forgiven and celebrated after all he has done. Then I remember that I do not deserve to be accepted and forgiven and celebrated by my Father God after all the sinful things I have done. Please forgive me, Father, for the times I have been like that older brother. Yes, I can identify with him.

Don't Miss the Party

It made him miss the party;
His feelings were so hurt.
His father had forgiven
The son all clothed in dirt.
While he had stayed and labored...
Had done a double share,
His brother played and partied
Without a single care.
It made him miss the party
Because he felt betrayed.
His brother had been pardoned
From all the mess he made.
Why should there be a party?
He could not understand.
Yet, Father gave the orders,
And said, "Strike up the band!"
It made him miss the party...
His jealousy and pride.
Acceptance of his brother
He just could not abide.
We often miss the party
When we pass up the chance
To celebrate redemption
And just get up and dance.

* *

Luke 15:25-28
"Meanwhile, the older son was in the field. When he came
near the house, he heard music and dancing. So he called
one of the servants and asked him what was going on. 'Your
brother has come,' he replied, 'and your father has killed the
fattened calf because he has him back safe and sound.'
"The older brother became angry and refused to go in.
So his father went out and pleaded with him.

* *

In the Eyes of the Beholder

For years my husband has wanted to buy some peacocks just for the enjoyment of watching them. He recently purchased three...a two-year-old male, a one-year-old male, and a one-year-old female. The older male already had his beautiful coloring that we associate with male peacocks. Unfortunately, he had to be put into a special crate to be transferred to his new home. During the trip, he moved around too much and messed up several of his feathers. Some of them were broken off, and some of them were bent in various directions. He was no longer quite as beautiful as he had been; however, he did not realize that fact. He continued to strut around and rustle his feathers in front of the peahen, totally unaware of his altered appearance. In his mind he was still as beautiful as ever. There were no mirrors or other judgmental peacocks to tell him otherwise.

How wonderful it would be if we could be just as oblivious to our scars and bruises and brokenness as that peacock. What if we had no hypercritical mirrors to reflect the pain and hardship we have endured throughout our earthly lives? What if we could just ignore remarks made by others who wish only to point out our shortcomings and who try to make us feel ugly? What if we could block out the hurtful darts fired from Satan's demons who keep trying to remind us of our sinful pasts which have already been cleansed by the blood of Jesus Christ? What if we all decided to see ourselves as God sees us...as His beautiful children made new again through the sacrifice of Jesus?

Yes, life has battered us from time to time, and we have a few, or maybe several, broken "feathers," but God knew that would happen when He sent us here. In His divine plan, He made a way for our renewal of mind, soul, and (eventually) body. We must see ourselves as God sees us and ignore worldly opinions about our lives. Let us try to have an attitude like that banged-up peacock and see ourselves as beautiful and worthy, because God has made us so. That came at a very great price that can never be forgotten.

* *

* *

Laundromat Reflection #1

Once more I received a pleasant surprise at the Laundromat. (It doesn't take very much to make me happy.) This time I was in Moundsville, West Virginia. I have an assembly line routine that I use when I go to a laundromat. First, I place the sorted laundry into the washing machines. Next, I pour in the liquid detergent. I close the lids and set the machines on the proper settings for the clothes inside. Lastly, I put the quarters in the slots, push them in, and listen to the machine start filling up with water.

This time, as I was moving from machine to machine to install the quarters into the slots, I reached the fourth machine and it was already full of seven quarters. It took me by surprise to see them there, and it took a few seconds for it to fully register. I am not sure if someone put them there, did not need as many washing machines as they thought they would need, and forgot to remove them, or if they were left there deliberately.

It came to my mind that it was a random act of kindness. I recalled the movie "Pay It Forward" and decided that was what some kind person was doing. I choose to believe that someone wanted to do something nice for whoever came behind her (or him) that morning. I love to do things like that myself, and it was a pleasant surprise to have someone do that for me.

Whether it was a mistake or a deliberate good deed, it was a small blessing either way---either a gift from God or a gift from a random stranger. Small blessings are so nice, but we must be on the alert to recognize them.

* *

2 Peter 1:5-7
For this very reason, make every effort to add to your faith goodness;
and to goodness, knowledge; and to knowledge self-control; and to
self-control, perseverance; and to perseverance, godliness; and to
godliness, brotherly kindness; and to brotherly kindness, love.

* *

Dead Limbs

Sometimes my mind wanders to strange thoughts. As I was sitting on our front porch one morning listening to the birds chirping, it occurred to me to wonder how dead limbs can be attached to live trees for extended periods of time. I also was thinking how useless dead limbs are. Then two more thoughts occurred to me. One thought was that even dead limbs are useful to the birds in our yard. They happily perch on those limbs and sing, sing, sing. It doesn't matter that those limbs are bare and have no beautiful foliage; they still serve a purpose as long as they are attached to the tree.

Secondly, I thought how we are often like those dead limbs. We are attached to the living body of Christ, yet we seem lifeless. We lose our zeal. We move in slow motion. We have no joy. Our faith seems to have only a faint heartbeat. We need a renewal before we completely die and fall away from the true source of life.

Unlike the dead limbs of trees, we cannot serve the purpose for which we were created if we are not filled with the life which we have been given. From time to time most of us go through periods of being "dead limbs"; but, unlike dead limbs on trees, we can be filled with life once again by going to the root of the tree of life...Jesus Christ. Through prayer and petition and thanksgiving, we can once more be filled with new life in our spirits. We can once again be useful and serve our God-given purpose in life. We can still become a beautiful branch in the body of God.

* *

John 15:5-8
"I am the vine; you are the branches. If a man remains in me and I in him, he will bear much fruit; apart from me you can do nothing. If anyone does not remain in me, he is like a branch that is thrown away and withers; such branches are picked up, thrown into the fire and burned. If you remain in me and my words remain in you, ask whatever you wish, and it will be given you. This is to my Father's glory, that you bear much fruit, showing yourselves to be my disciples."

* *

The Ivy Leaf

One lone, little ivy leaf proudly holds itself erect in a flowerpot on a table beside my recliner. I have carefully tended that small leaf for the past eight months as we have been living in a travel trailer near my husband's job location. It was taken from a plant that was given to me when my father died, and it makes me feel closer to Daddy when I look at it. Actually, I brought two leaves with me in a small container of potting soil, but one of them did not survive. It was cast away.

It is important to me that I keep a part of that plant alive. This little leaf has traveled from Louisiana to West Virginia and even been accidentally dumped out onto the floor once, but it is still growing. Hopefully, one day it will put out more leaves and become like its mother plant and can be shared with others. It has prevailed through all of its trials.

Our faith is a lot like that little ivy leaf. It is derived from a "mother faith" that was taught to us by someone who took the time to plant the seed of faith within us. Eventually, though, we had to be transplanted and begin growing on our own. It is a slow and sometimes painful process, and often it seems we will not survive; but our Father made us strong and is always with us to help us get our roots firmly established in His will. If we are willing, He will prune us and shape us to His will. As our faith begins to grow and blossom, we will find that we have enough to share with someone else. We can give them a "leaf of faith" to start them on their way.

Unfortunately, there is also faith that is founded on rocky, shallow ground and cannot survive. Perhaps it was never really faith at all. Just as the second leaf withered and died, so will a faith that is not fed with God's Word and watered with prayer. Both leaves had the same opportunity to grow. One did, but the other did not. Perhaps the leaves could not actually choose their own destinies, but we can. God wants us to continue to grow in our faith and to share that faith with others. We must be branches of the One True Vine. We must learn to "grow where we are planted."

* *

John 15: 5-6

"I am the vine; you are the branches. If a man remains in me and I in him, he will bear much fruit; apart from me you can do nothing. If anyone does not remain in me, he is like a branch that is thrown away and withers; such branches are picked up, thrown into the fire and burned."

* *

I'M GONNA TELL MY DADDY!

Just before my fifth birthday I was diagnosed with polio. As I wrote in my first book, everything turned out well from that experience, but I recall one memory that I have always carried with me from there. When I was first taken to a hospital for tests, I fell asleep and awoke to find myself "hog-tied" with my knees pulled up against my neck and tied securely so that I was unable to move. Nurses were securing me in position, and a doctor was sticking a needle into my back. I had no idea what a spinal tap was; I only knew that I was terrified!

I remember seeing my mother standing nearby, so I deduced that she would be of no help to get me out of that situation. Little did they know that I had a "backup" who I was certain would rescue me. I remember screaming over and over at the top of my lungs, "I'm gonna tell my daddy! I'm gonna tell my daddy!" (I am a true Southerner, so I still catch myself saying "gonna" instead of "going to.") I was certain that my daddy would come to my rescue. I could always count on that.

I found out later that my daddy was just outside the doors and could hear me, but of course he could not stop the procedure. I think how that must have hurt him to hear me calling for him when he knew that they were just trying to help me. I realize now that sometimes we have to be hurt in order to be helped. That seems like the supreme oxymoron, but it is true.

That experience brings to my mind how, when things in life go wrong, we run to tell our Heavenly Father. With childlike assurance, we instinctively know that He will always protect us and punish those who harm us. That is not to say that we will never hurt or have problems. Jesus assures us in *John 16:33* that *"I have told you these things, so that in me you may have peace. In this world you will have trouble. But take heart! I have overcome the world."*

Sometimes we make our own trouble through our disobedience. Those are some of the times when we must hurt in order to be helped. Unfortunately, we humans often must learn lessons the hard way. Yet, through those experiences, we learn to be obedient. Just as our earthly parents corrected us sternly, but with much love, so does our Heavenly Father. We often need "tough love." Still, whenever we humbly run to our Father God with tears streaming down our faces because we have been hurt, or sometimes with a feeling of shame for something we have done, He lifts us up in His arms, wipes away our tears, and assures us that everything will be okay. In my mind I can often hear Him say, "Don't worry! I've got it covered!"

I was one of the fortunate ones, or perhaps I would best be described as one of the "blessed" ones, who had a daddy I could always count on to "have my back" no matter what I did. My daddy is now with my Heavenly Father; so now, when I feel the world is treating me unfairly, I say, "I'm gonna tell my Father!" I *know* He has me covered!

* *

Psalm 91:2, 4
I will say of the LORD, "He is my refuge and my fortress, my God, in whom I trust." He will cover you with his feathers, and under his wings you will find refuge; his faithfulness will be your shield and rampart.

Psalm 32:1-2
Blessed is he whose transgressions are forgiven, whose sins are covered. Blessed is the man whose sin the LORD does not count against him and in whose spirit is no deceit.

* *

Sweet Conversation

One night at a church supper, I was blessed to have the company of a sweet thirteen-year-old young man sitting across from my husband and me. He is a handsome, alert young man who is also autistic. Sometimes he just likes to talk, and his wisdom astounds me.

During that particular conversation, he asked me what happens when we sin. I explained that we ask God for forgiveness, which he mercifully grants to us, and then we strive to do better. I also told him that we will still slip-up from time to time, but God will keep forgiving us when we ask. He looked at me and said, "He's a busy God!" That observant statement was the inspiration for the following poem.

* *

Matthew 11:25-26
At that time Jesus said, "I praise you, Father, Lord of heaven and earth, because you have hidden these things from the wise and learned, and revealed them to little children. Yes, Father, for this was your good pleasure.

* *

Busy God

Oh, Father, please forgive me,
For I have failed once more;
And I'm here, as you can see,
To knock on mercy's door.
How many times I've knelt here,
I can no longer count.
I have a need to draw near
To drink from mercy's fount.
It's hard to imagine how
You hear so many pleas
As every moment heads bow
And millions hit their knees.
I am not the only one
Who comes to plead my case.
It's through the work of your Son
My sins you can erase.
It must make you glad to hear
Your children when we pray,
As you face from year to year
Another busy day.

* *

Ephesians 3:12
In him and through faith in him we may approach
God with freedom and confidence.

1 John 1:9
If we confess our sins, he is faithful and just and will forgive
us our sins and purify us from all unrighteousness.

* *

Ezekiel 34:26
I will make them and the places surrounding
my hill a blessing. I will send down showers in
season; there will be showers of blessing.

Living in Clover

Four-leaf clovers have always fascinated me. It isn't that I believe in "luck," because I know my fate is defined by the master plan of my Master. Actually, the four-leaf clovers remind me of my Maker and of how He sends special things our way when we often don't take the time to notice them. Sometimes they are very tiny reminders that He is always watching us and that He wants the very best for our lives. How many times do we miss his gentle reminders?

One morning I found two four-leaf clovers in a field close to our campsite when my husband was working in Illinois for a short time. We had both found some four-leaf clovers there prior to that morning, and that particular field seemed to have a bountiful supply. For some reason, on that morning, I began to wonder if there were any such thing as a five-leaf clover. I had never heard of one, but I had found a clover in that same field that was two three-leaf clovers growing on the same stem. It had six leaves---three on the right side and three on the left side. I found that to be rather interesting. Somehow two clovers had merged into one, but a five-leaf clover would really be something unusual.

The very next morning, I found a five-leaf clover near the same spot I had found some of the other clovers. It was as if God were telling me, "Yes, I hear your thoughts and send more blessings on my people than they ever fully realize. Please take the time to look for them."

I know that I am a silly old woman with crazy ideas sometimes, but God doesn't seem to mind. He answers prayers that are not actually put into words, but He wants to assure us that He is always aware of our every thought. Whether a clover has three, four, five, or six leaves, it can serve as a reminder for us to be aware that we have a Savior who is closer than a brother. We have a God who loves us beyond measure, just as the clovers in the fields are too many to count.

"Living in clover" means "living in prosperity or in pleasant circumstances," according to the Merriam-Webster dictionary. Even when we are not rich in the eyes of the world, we are rich in the eyes of God. We are His children, His heirs, the ones He loves more than anything else He has ever created. We have a home in the City of Gold that no one can ever take away from us. We have been assured that, even if we lose everything in this world, we will gain everything in Heaven. We are going to have the only home that really matters in the only world that really matters. We are living in clover.

* *

Proverbs 15:3
The eyes of the LORD are everywhere, keeping
watch on the wicked and the good.

* *

The Porch Light

When I was young and was out at night for any reason, I could always depend on the fact that our porch light would be burning when I returned. Recently I started thinking about that porch light and what it meant to me. I did not realize it at the time, but it meant security and love. Someone was there waiting for my return and praying for my safety. Someone was waiting up to make sure I made it home. Someone loved me.

Now, as my years in this world rapidly increase, I can almost see another porch light shining off in the distance. God has had it burning since my journey here began, and it will continue to shine until I go home to stay. Just like the light on the porch of my childhood home, that Heavenly light is a reminder that I am loved, I don't have to fear, and that Someone is interceding on my behalf. He has promised that the bulb will never burn out and that He will be waiting up for me when I get home.

* *

Psalm 119:105
Your word is a lamp to my feet and a light for my path.

* *

God's Porch Light

When God sent me here some time ago,
He left the porch light on.
I have traveled through this world below,
But I've not been alone.
I have known some happiness and pain
And love along the way.
I have suffered loss and enjoyed gain
And felt great need to pray.
Like someone lost in a cold, dark cave,
I have prayed for a torch.
One day I'll see, far beyond my grave,
The light on God's front porch.

* *

Revelation 21:23
*The city does not need the sun or the moon to shine on it, for
the glory of God gives it light, and the Lamb is its lamp.*

* *

James 1:12
Blessed is the one who perseveres under trial because,
having stood the test, that person will receive the crown
of life that the Lord has promised to those who love him.

Leaning Angel with a Broken Wing

There is a large concrete angel in our front yard. She is missing her left wing from a tumble she took several years ago. The angel also leans several degrees to her left because she sits on un-level ground. She is stained and dirty from years of weathering this world's storms. How I so often can relate to that angel.

As we travel throughout life, we sometimes get broken. At times we become stained and dirty. We often travel on un-level ground; yet, we must do our best to keep standing. Ephesians 6:13 directs us to *"Therefore put on the full armor of God, so that when the day of evil comes, you may be able to stand your ground, and after you have done everything, to stand."* Sometimes we have to try to fly with a "missing wing." Jesus warned us of such happenings in John 16:33 when He said, *"I have told you these things, so that in me you may have peace. In this world you will have trouble. But take heart! I have overcome the world."*

Sometimes I get so angry at Satan when I see all of the destruction he does in the lives of God's children. I am looking forward to the day when I can watch Satan's ultimate defeat and he will no longer have any power in this world. I can understand how people who do not know the Lord can be so easily swayed by Satan's wiles. It is hard enough to be strong and alert when we as Christians (God's adopted children) are confronted with Satan's temptations, strategies, and condemnation. He knows just where to hit us in our most vulnerable places...quite often through our children and grandchildren...the most innocent of us. Many of my friends and family members struggle on a day-by-day basis because of choices they made years ago. We all have hurts, habits, and hang-ups. We all must fight our battles; but, in the grand scheme of things, it is worth every bruised and broken part and the scars of our battles with sin. We must remember the promise we find in Romans 8:16-17: *"The Spirit himself testifies with our spirit that we are God's children. Now if we are children, then we are heirs---heirs of God and co-heirs with Christ, if indeed we share in his sufferings in order that we may also share in his glory."*

AMEN

Never an Orphan

After months of upheaval over the illness and death of our mama, I am once again finding peace and solace as I sit on our front porch and gaze at the wonder of God's creations. Birds are flitting around singing praises to their Maker without a care as they send me a message that all is still right with the world as long as God is on His throne.

Over the past thirteen years since we lost our daddy, I have often wondered how it would feel to be an orphan when we lost Mama. Now I realize that I can never become an orphan because my Heavenly Father has always been and will always be. He gave me the wonderful earthly parents that I had in order to show me a tiny glimpse of what He is like. Since I would rate Mama and Daddy as "tens" on an earthly scale, God's rating as a loving parent would have to go to infinity.

It has been said many times by many people that it is impossible to understand how people get through times of great loss if they don't know God. I agree. If I did not have the assurance that we will all meet again without the fear of another parting, I could never feel the "peace that surpasses all understanding" that God has given me during this time. Yes, I hurt, and I know there will be days when I will hurt even more than I do now. I know that I am still a little numb from it all, and that is God's way of caring for me at this time. Would I love to have Mama back here with us? For my sake, yes; for her sake, no. She made it plain that she was ready to go home, and that is all that matters. Our parents guided us throughout our lives in one way or another, and they have both shown us the path that leads to the home we are all meant to inhabit. What a reunion that will be when we arrive at our destination and find them waiting there with open arms. At last we will be in the presence of all three of our parents for eternity.

* *

John 14:18
I will not leave you as orphans; I will come to you.

* *

Thought Number One

When Adam and Eve walked away from the garden, a multitude of men and women followed them.

When Christ walked up Calvary's hill, He walked alone.

When Christ walked out of the tomb, a multitude of men and women followed Him.

Ecclesiastes 3:11(a)
He has made everything beautiful in its time.

Another Lesson from Peacocks

It is amazing the things I am learning from our peacocks. First, I learned that beauty truly is in the eyes of the beholder. Now I have proof that beauty is only skin deep, as the old saying goes. I don't know how many of you are familiar with the sound made by peacocks, but I can assure you that it is not all that pleasant. No matter how beautiful the outside of a peacock may be, what comes out of his mouth certainly is not melodious.

I know some people like that. They are absolutely beautiful on the outside (by earthly standards), but what comes out of them when they open their mouths is extremely ugly. Every word they speak is criticism of everyone and everything, bigotry, lies, condemnation of others, "oh, woe is me," gossip, boasting of self, etc. They are the people no one wants to be around because they make us feel very annoyed and very depressed. They can really bring us down on a "sunshiny day."

In 1 Peter 3:3-4, we read *"Your beauty should not come from outward adornment, such as braided hair and the wearing of gold jewelry and fine clothes. Instead, it should be that of your inner self, the unfading beauty of a gentle and quiet spirit, which is of great worth in God's sight."* I don't think this implies that we should not wear jewelry or fine clothes or a little makeup if it makes us feel better about ourselves; however, we must not depend on such things for our genuine beauty. Proverbs 31:30 directs us that *"Charm is deceptive, and beauty is fleeting; but a woman who fears the LORD is to be praised."*

From 1 Peter 3:10 we learn that *"Whoever would love life and see good days must keep his tongue from evil and his lips from deceitful speech."* In James 3:8-10 we are told *"but no man can tame the tongue. It is a restless evil, full of deadly poison. With the tongue we praise our Lord and Father, and with it we curse men, who have been made in God's likeness. Out of the same mouth come praise and cursing. My brothers, this should not be."*

I don't know if peacocks are guilty of speaking evil, but I do think they are guilty of boasting about their beauty...at least that is how it appears to me. I know that I have been guilty of many of the things I listed above, and it is a daily struggle to keep a rein on what comes out of my mouth. That is why one prayer that I repeat quite often comes from Psalm 19:14. *"May the words of my mouth and the meditation of my heart be pleasing in your sight, O LORD, my Rock and my Redeemer."*

AMEN

Pitching Washers

Back in the "olden days" when life was much simpler than it has been for a long time, sometimes when the farm work was done and there were a few idle hours for visiting, the men would sit out on our front steps and pitch flat round washers at a small hole they had dug into the ground a few feet from where they sat. I guess it could be called the lazy man's version of pitching horseshoes. The object of the game, of course, was to throw the washer into the hole or get it as close to the hole as he could.

I was a young girl and had a great desire to play the game, too. My daddy told me, "No," which was a word I seldom heard from him. After repeated requests to let me play and repeated denials, I decided that, if I could not play, then neither could they. I sat down right on top of that little hole in the ground and refused to move. My daddy was a man who spoiled me rotten, but he was also a man who did not tell me something over and over again. When he told me to move, he intended for me to move! I refused, and that led to one of about three spankings my daddy ever gave me. He did not "beat" me by any stretch of the imagination, but he did "correct" me. I remember that correction to this very day, more than fifty years later.

Sometimes God tells us "No" for our own good, but we insist on having our own way. Sometimes He gives us more than one warning, and we still refuse to comply with his advice. Eventually, He "corrects" us. Often that correction comes in the form of our having to suffer the consequences of our disobedience. God corrects us because He loves us and wants the best for us. His way is always the best way, but unfortunately it sometimes takes us a while to figure that out. If we insist on having our way, then He will often comply as He sits back and watches us learn things the hard way. Those are the lessons we remember more than fifty years later, or however long we live in this world.

What if God told us, "It's My way or the highway"? What if

we had no second chance...or third chance...etc...? As much as my earthly father always forgave my disobedience, my Heavenly Father forgives me even more. *1John 1:9* assures us that *"If we confess our sins, he is faithful and just and will forgive us our sins and purify us from all unrighteousness."* Sometimes, when God throws "washers of blessings" my way, it seems that I "sit on the hole" and won't let them in. That is my loss. That is my lesson to be learned. Sometimes I just have to learn it the hard way.

* *

Romans 10:21(b)
"All day long I have held out my hands to a disobedient and obstinate people."

* *

Psalm 63:8
I cling to you; your right hand upholds me.

Two Trees

When I was a young girl, there were two trees in our yard that were twisted around one another as if in a lovers' embrace. They were not very big trees, and I don't know what kind of trees they were; but that doesn't really matter.

I am not sure when or why I first noticed how those trees were so closely intertwined, but for some reason they fascinated me. I once wrote a poem about those trees for a high school English class. There was something rather touching about their "relationship."

Now, for some reason, my memory has recalled the image of those trees. Today I think of them as a symbol of what our relationship with Christ should be. We should be standing so closely to Him that, as we grow in our knowledge of him, our entire beings should become entwined with His...all of our hearts, souls, and minds. How wonderful it would be if we would all be so joined to Christ that it would be impossible to tell where one ends and the other begins. If only God's people would truly be "God's people" in every sense of the word, what a wonderful world this could be.

* *

Proverbs 18:24
A man of many companions may come to ruin, but there is a friend who sticks closer than a brother.

Psalm 65:4
Blessed are those you choose and bring near to live in your courts! We are filled with the good things of your house, of your holy temple.

* *

The Tree

There is a small ash tree in our front yard. I have spent many hours on our front porch, and that tree is always in my line of sight as I gaze out toward my right. That little tree has been struck by lightning twice and sprayed with poison from an errant crop-dusting plane on at least one occasion. Still, it struggles to survive.

The west side of the tree that faces away from our house took the hardest hit from the lightning and the poison. Therefore, that half of the tree is made up mostly of very thin branches with a scattering of tiny leaves while the east side of the tree is lush with green foliage. My husband has wanted to cut it down a few times, but I always talk him out of it. I think it needs every chance to survive because it never gives up.

That little tree reminds me of my life. I came into this world all vigorous and unscathed, ready to take on the world and all of its obstacles, much as the east side of that tree. As the years quickly passed, however, I soon discovered that this world is full of dangers and snares that leave scars that stay with us for this lifetime, as illustrated by the west side of the tree. Yet, our God never cuts us down and throws us away.

I love the idea that, even though we become frail and not so beautiful anymore according to man's standards, we are forever beautiful in our Maker's eyes. This life does take its toll on us if we hang around on earth long enough; but one day when we become born again into His kingdom, we will be vigorous and unscathed once more. At this stage of my life, I am more like the west side of that tree, but I know that "soon and very soon" I will be as brand new.

* *

Revelation 21:5
He who was seated on the throne said, "I am making
everything new!" Then he said, "Write this down,
for these words are trustworthy and true."

* *

Me, Myself And I

2 Timothy 2:15
Do your best to present yourself to
God as one approved, a worker who
does not need to be ashamed and who
correctly handles the word of truth.

My Treasure

My idea of treasure
    has changed throughout the years,
And I've learned that pleasure
    might cost a pool of tears.
Some lessons I have learned
    were taught in a "hard way."
How often I've been burned
    with a high price to pay.
Things that used to matter
    no longer mean a thing;
They're just noise and clatter,
    and have no joy to bring.
I've learned what really counts
    and that God's Word is true,
And I try to renounce
    my worldly point of view.
Soon there will be no trace
    of earth's richest measure,
And Heaven is the place
    I hope to find my treasure.

* *

Matthew 6:19-21
*"Do not store up for yourselves treasures on earth, where moth
and rust destroy, and where thieves break in and steal. But store
up for yourselves treasures in heaven, where moth and rust
do not destroy, and where thieves do not break in and steal.
For where your treasure is, there your heart will be also."*

* *

My Golden Calves

"I threw the gold into the fire, and out came this calf!"
When I read what Aaron said, I just had to laugh.
The image of such an event was just too absurd.
Ridiculous! Such an excuse I had never heard.
I wonder what God must have thought about that excuse.
Did that explain that golden calf they chose to produce?
But then I thought of many times I had done the same,
When I had formed an alibi to conceal my shame.
That lie I told was very small, and you understand,
That gossip which passed from my lips was just secondhand.
I know I went into a place I should not be seen,
But it really did no harm; you know what I mean.
When someone told that dirty joke, I did not complain;
Those people know what I believe...I need not explain.
Some segments of that show I watched portrayed a dirty scene,
But it's so hard this day and time to find one that's clean.
A dirty word came from my mouth; it just slipped right out.
You know that I don't speak that way...how did that come about?
I know I should have been in church, but it was not my fault.
I said a prayer and thanked you for all those fish I caught.
You know that I work hard all week, and I need some rest.
I cannot be my cheery self if I get too stressed.
I spent part of the ten percent that should have gone to you;
But, Lord, you know how much I owe, and bills were coming due.
A friend asked me to say a prayer and please not to forget,
But I have been so busy, Lord, I have not done that yet.
As I look back, I realize what I've always known.
The golden calves throughout my life were made by me alone.

Exodus 32:2-4a

Aaron answered them, "Take off the gold earrings that your wives, your sons and your daughters are wearing, and bring them to me." So all the people took off their earrings and brought them to Aaron. He took what they handed him and made it into an idol cast in the shape of a calf, fashioning it with a tool.

Exodus 32:22-24

"Do not be angry, my lord," Aaron answered. "You know how prone these people are to evil. They said to me, 'Make us gods who will go before us. As for this fellow Moses who brought us up out of Egypt, we don't know what has happened to him.' So I told them, 'Whoever has any gold jewelry, take it off.' Then they gave me the gold, and I threw it into the fire, and out came this calf!"

My Mind

God knows my thoughts; that causes me concern;
For in my mind He might find things unclean.
Some trash creeps in I must take out and burn---
Some evil thoughts, some ugly, and some mean.
I wish I could replace the bad with good
And only think of love and trust and hope;
But it appears from time to time I should
Wash out my mind with a large bar of soap!

* *

Matthew 9:4
*Knowing their thoughts, Jesus said, "Why do you
entertain evil thoughts in your hearts?"*

Hebrews 3:1
*Therefore, holy brothers, who share in the heavenly calling, fix your
thoughts on Jesus, the apostle and high priest whom we confess.*

* *

My Fig Leaf

When I see my reflection
And see my guilt and shame,
With every recollection,
I know I am to blame.
My first thought is to quickly
Disguise the things I've done.
I must not let my God see
I am the guilty one.
We humans want sins covered---
Adam and Eve tried it;
But just as they discovered,
My fig leaf does not fit.

* *

Genesis 2:25
Adam and his wife were both naked, and they felt no shame.

Genesis 3:7
*Then the eyes of both of them were opened, and they
realized they were naked; so they sewed fig leaves
together and made coverings for themselves.*

* *

My Mouth

My mouth is a useful part of me,
Of that I have no doubt.
It's a part of my anatomy
That I can't live without.
I would think that such a simple thing
That's really very small
Could never cause a painful sting
Or any harm at all.
But so many times throughout my years
I've proven that untrue.
My mouth has caused some hurtful tears
When words just slipped right through.
Sometimes I do not stop to think
Before I start to speak.
I did not know how some words can stink
And really start to reek!
Quite often it's been my desire
To take back what I said;
Words can cause damage like a fire,
And quickly they can spread.
I pray one day that I will learn,
Although the lesson's hard.
May I speak with love and real concern
As every word I guard.

* *

Psalm 141:3
Set a guard over my mouth, O LORD;
keep watch over the door of my lips.

* *

My Offerings

Do my offerings give off a pleasant scent?
Do I use my gifts in ways that honor Him?
Or have I learned to sit and be content
To hide my lamp until its light grows dim?
Does my Lord find some pleasure when I bring
The harvest of the fruit from all my seeds?
Or do I disappoint my holy King
By letting all my gifts grow up in weeds?
The talents that He gives are mine to use,
And often I forget to stop and think
That what I make of them is mine to choose.
Do they smell sweet, or do my offerings stink?

* *

Philippians 4:18
I have received full payment and have more than enough.
I am amply supplied, now that I have received from
Epaphroditus the gifts you sent. They are a fragrant
offering, an acceptable sacrifice, pleasing to God.

* *

My Shopping Cart

When I see a shopping cart, God gently brings to mind
Many things I'm thankful for and how He's been so kind.
Sometimes my life feels empty as I walk down life's aisles,
But one by one God's blessings begin to come in piles.
He sends me bags of mercy from His storehouse of grace,
And then He adds forgiveness and healing by the case.
A big box of happiness, He's placed there just for me;
It's wrapped with much compassion and joy and charity.
My shopping cart is filled with God's blessings and His love,
But His gift of salvation is what I'm proudest of.
So, now I am reminded each time I push a cart
That God can fill all of me...especially my heart.

* *

Ezekiel 34:26
*I will make them and the places surrounding my hill a blessing. I will
send down showers in season; there will be showers of blessing.*

* *

Country Girl

I thank you, God, for making me
A country girl as all can see.
I do not think that I could bear
To see big crowds just everywhere.
The grass is green, the sky is blue,
And everywhere I can see You.
I love to see the spaces wide,
Not all closed in on every side.
I love the rivers and the trees,
The daffodils and honeybees.
I thrive on air so clean and free;
A city girl I could not be.
A city has too many frills;
I'd rather have the rolling hills.
I see my friends and stop to talk,
And signs don't always read, "Don't walk!"
I never have to be afraid
To check the door or lift the shade.
The sunlight fills up every room,
And in the spring the flowers bloom.
I'm just as happy as can be
You made a country girl of me.

* *

Psalm 107:1
Give thanks to the LORD, for he is good; his love endures forever.

* *

Pray Until Something Happens

Colossians 4:2
Devote yourselves to prayer, being
watchful and thankful.

Call Home

Most parents tell their children wherever they might roam,
"When you get where you're going, be sure you call back home."
They want to know you arrived at your destination
And that you are safe and sound in that situation.
They assure you constantly that they will always care;
And if you have some trouble, they'll surely be right there.
You will have many journeys on which you'll slip and fall;
So, anytime you need them, just make that homeward call.

Our Father up in Heaven tells us to do the same.
We can call Him when we're proud or when we're filled with shame.
He wants to hear everything, all the good and the bad.
He wants to share our laughter and hold us when we're sad.
He's such a loving parent; we're always on his mind,
For we are all his children, each carefully designed.
He's waiting so patiently while in this world we roam,
And it makes Him so happy when his children call home.

* *

Jeremiah 33:3
'Call to me and I will answer you and tell you great
and unsearchable things you do not know.'

* *

Glue Me, Lord

Glue me, Lord, to the narrow road;
Keep my footsteps straight.
When I stumble beneath a load,
Help me with that weight.

Glue me, Lord, to your wounded side,
You who understands,
For you yourself was crucified
With your nail-pierced hands.

Glue me, Lord, to your Holy Word
And all its power,
For through its message You are heard
In each sweet hour.

Glue me, Lord, with your truth and might
And your loving way.
Please keep me always in your sight
And don't let me stray.

****

Proverbs 18:24
*A man of many companions may come to ruin, but
there is a friend who sticks closer than a brother.*

****

The Answer to a Prayer

You may not have money or fame or such,
And you may not think your life is worth much.
Perhaps you may think your talents are small
And could not make much difference at all.

But you have a smile worth more than you think
To brighten a day---as quick as a wink.
A kind word from you might just do the trick
To lift up low spirits or help heal the sick.

Encouragement may be what you do best
Or lending a hand without a request.
You might testify how God's brought you through
And thus help someone who's feeling quite blue.

You might teach a class or read to a child
Or make one feel welcomed because you just smiled.
Someone may have prayed for someone to care,
And you could just be their answer to prayer.

* *

Ezra 8:23
So we fasted and petitioned our God about
this, and he answered our prayer.

* *

Ezekiel 22:30
"I looked for a man among them who would build up the wall and stand before me in the gap on behalf of the land so I would not have to destroy it, but I found none."

Standing in the Gap

Sometimes the gap seems ten feet wide
With muddy slopes that slip and slide.
Then I begin to wonder why
I ever thought that I should try
To fill the space with fervent prayer
When others seem just not to care.
What makes me think that I can fill
That space that spans from hill to hill?
No one should have to stand alone
And reach from earth to Heaven's throne.
So, though the gap is hard to span,
I'll do the very best I can,
And trust that God will do the rest
To help my friend endure this test.

* *

Romans 8:26
*In the same way, the Spirit helps us in our weakness. We
do not know what we ought to pray for, but the Spirit
himself intercedes for us through wordless groans.*

* *

PSALM 23

The Lord---the only true, living one
Is my Shepherd---this can't be un-done.
I shall not want---I get His best.
He makes me lie down---He gives me rest.
He leads me to peace---as He stands guard.
He restores my soul---when life gets hard.
He guides me---He shows paths not to take.
I try to do right---for His name's sake.
When I walk through the shadows---of death,
I'll praise Him---with my very last breath.
I will fear no evil---He's with me.
He protects and comforts---enemies flee.
He prepares a table---I'm His guest.
He anoints me with oil---it's His best.
My cup overflows---He blesses me
With goodness and love---eternally.
I'll be at home---never to sever
In the house of the LORD---forever.

PSALM 23---VERSION 2

You are my Shepherd, and I am your lamb;
My protection comes from the great "I Am."
You love and console me---meet every need;
My wish is to follow as you gently lead.
Each day new blessings on me you outpour;
In quiet hours my soul you restore.
I rest beside rivers and drink my fill;
All I desire is to do my Lord's will.
And when I walk through that valley of death,
I'll praise your name as I take my last breath.
As you hold me closely, I will not fear,
Even with my mortal enemies near.
My table is waiting---it's been reserved.
I'll share in your bounty---so undeserved.
I have more blessings than my cup can hold,
With mercy and goodness and love untold.
Your home will be mine; you're my truest friend.
I'll dwell with you there for days without end.

Obstructions

Lord, I want to talk to You, but life gets in the way.
Lord, I want to hear from You and learn the things You say.
Lord, I want to do what's right, but sometimes I do not.
Lord, I want to come to You without one sinful spot.
Lord, I want to feel You near though sometimes I might move.
Lord, I want to do the things that I know You approve.
Lord, I want to feel secure and trust You to provide.
Lord, I want to face my fears, not run away and hide.
Lord, I want to feel my faith grow stronger day by day.
Lord, I want to do Your will, but I get in the way.

* *

Romans 7:21-25(a)
*So I find this law at work: When I want to do good, evil is
right there with me. For in my inner being I delight in God's
law; but I see another law at work in the members of my body,
waging war against the law of my mind and making me a
prisoner of the law of sin at work within my members. What
a wretched man I am! Who will rescue me from this body of
death? Thanks be to God---through Jesus Christ our Lord!*

* *

Determination

I will sit here, Lord, until I hear you speak.
I will stay here, Lord, 'til I find what I seek.
I will wait here, Lord, until the time is right.
I will kneel here, Lord, throughout this long dark night.
I will trust you, Lord, when earthly things seem bleak.
I will march on, Lord, although my body's weak.
I will praise you, Lord, throughout both joy and pain.
I will thank you, Lord, for sunshine and for rain.
I will serve you, Lord, and be your helping hand.
I will follow, Lord, when I don't understand.
I will share you, Lord, with people that I meet.
I will love you, Lord, until my last heartbeat.

* *

Romans 4:20-21
Yet he did not waver through unbelief regarding the promise of
God, but was strengthened in his faith and gave glory to God, being
fully persuaded that God had power to do what he had promised.

* *

It's been dark for a long time, Lord.

I KNOW

Where is the light?

I KNOW

I need to see a glimmer of it.

I KNOW

---

2 Corinthians 4:6
For God, who said, "Let light shine out of darkness," made his light shine in our hearts to give us the light of the knowledge of God's glory displayed in the face of Christ.

His Plan Is on the Way

When problems come my way
And creep into my mind,
They're never here to stay
For God is much too kind
To let them hang around
And spoil the day He made
And steal the peace I've found
When sunlight turns to shade.
When I tell Him about
How life is treating me,
And I see no way out
But just calamity,
He tells me every time
That I should never fear
The mountains I must climb
For He is always near.
He's always in the lead
Before I kneel and pray.
Before I start to plead,
His plan is on the way.

* *

Daniel 9: 23(a)
As soon as you began to pray, an answer was given, which
I have come to tell you, for you are highly esteemed.

* *

This Christmas

I wish this Christmas could be what it really should be
Without the hustle and bustle and noise
Without the yearning and burning for toys
Without the hurry and worry and stress
Without the "need to" and "want to" impress.

I wish this Christmas could be what it really should be
Without the doom and gloom of bills
Without the need and greed and frills
Without the wear and tear on nerves
With all the honor it deserves.

I wish this Christmas could be what it really should be
A time of thanking God above
A time of never-ending love
A time to celebrate Christ's birth
A time of peace and joy on earth.

I wish this Christmas could be what it really should be.

* *

Luke 2:10-12
But the angel said to them, "Do not be afraid. I bring you
good news of great joy that will be for all the people. Today
in the town of David a Savior has been born to you; he is
Christ the Lord. This will be a sign to you: You will find
a baby wrapped in cloths and lying in a manger."

* *

I Wish

I wish our children could know some of our "good old days."
I wish for simpler times and some "good old-fashioned ways."
I wish we would not overlook the filth we see and hear.
I wish our leaders did not feel the need to interfere.
I wish that every family had a mom and a dad.
I wish each child could feel the love that I've always had.
I wish there were no drugs around sold out on the street.
I wish there were more people who simply will not cheat.
I wish that people would not use our Lord's name in vain.
I wish there were no violence that causes so much pain.
I wish that all profanity would just disappear.
I wish that half the world did not have to live in fear.
I wish that politicians would be honest and fair.
I wish more would be willing to kneel down in prayer.
I wish all of God's creatures were treated with respect.
I wish those frail and helpless would never feel neglect.
I wish all of God's children could have enough to eat.
I wish they all had shelter and shoes upon their feet.
I wish our world could be as God meant for it to be.
I wish we could live in peace with all humanity.
I wish everyone could know about God's love and grace.
I hope I will leave this world a little better place.

* *

Romans 12:12-13
Be joyful in hope, patient in affliction, faithful in prayer. Share
with God's people who are in need. Practice hospitality.

* *

Father, May I Have a Dime?

How often do I meekly go before God's throne of grace
And behave like some intruder afraid to show my face?
Why do I think I'll bother Him, with what I need to ask?
Why should the God of all the world assist me with my task?
The Bible says to boldly go and make our wishes known,
For He who owns the universe is sitting on that throne.
He's waiting to hear my request at any given time.
He offers everything, and yet, I settle for a dime.

* *

Hebrews 4:16
*Let us then approach the throne of grace with confidence, so that we
may receive mercy and find grace to help us in our time of need.*

Matthew 7:9-11
*Which of you, if his son asks for bread, will give him a stone? Or if
he asks for a fish will give him a snake? If you, then, though you are
evil, know how to give good gifts to your children, how much more
will your Father in heaven give good gifts to those who ask him!*

* *

Pray for the Little Things

Why does it seem so natural to pray when big storms arise,
As we cry out to our Savior when life's boat starts to capsize?
But what about the little storms that so often hide our sun?
The things that try to wash away all our happiness and fun?
Why do we think God does not care about each little worry?
Do we not want to bother Him? Is God in some big hurry?
Perhaps we feel our little hurts just could not really matter
To One who made the universe and caused sin's plans to shatter.
Is our God's time so limited---maybe His hours numbered?
If we ask one more thing of Him, will He be too encumbered?
Are our Lord's arms not strong enough? His shoulders just too narrow?
Does He not care for all of us? The One who feeds the sparrow?
Why can't we humans understand that God wants to be a part
Of every aspect of our lives---especially heart-to-heart.
When we are hurt, He feels our pain, for He once became a man
And lived within this sinful world to fulfill God's holy plan.
He had to face the things we face, and He felt the way we feel
When life is so discouraging and our suffering so real.
So, nothing's insignificant when we go to Him in prayer.
He's waiting very patiently just to hear our every care.

* *

1 Peter 5:7
Cast all your anxiety on him because he cares for you.

* *

Knee Time

It's been too long since I have knelt in prayer,
And though God hears my prayers from anywhere,
While walking, lying down, or sitting up,
With any meal or morning coffee cup,
God understands my heart's true condition,
No matter when or where or position;
But often I have much too much "me time."
Instead of "He time," "we time," and "knee time."

* *

Luke 22:41-42
*He withdrew about a stone's throw beyond them, **knelt***
***down and prayed**, "Father, if you are willing, take this*
cup from me; yet not my will, but yours be done."

* *

Satan Is A Liar

John 8:44(b)
He was a murderer from the beginning,
not holding to the truth, for there
is no truth in him. When he lies, he
speaks his native language, for he
is a liar and the father of lies.

Facing the Devil

Sometimes I feel as if I face the devil every day.
Temptations try to lure me as I go along my way.
I have to guard my thoughts, and I must watch the words I say.
The lion prowls around me as he hunts for his next prey.

When my life seems to be calm and peace comes gently flowing,
I get turned around again and don't know where I'm going.
Then Satan sends confusion with lies that just keep growing.
He piles on disappointments to hurts that I am towing.

The devil can be handsome when he covers up his lies,
And he is so attractive when he puts on his disguise.
I've learned to stand up to him as I look into his eyes,
For there I see his true self as I watch his temper rise.

This earth is now his kingdom, but it won't be very long.
One day I'll see my Savior casting out the evil throng.
Satan will be sent to hell where such wicked things belong
So, until that promised day, with God's help I will stay strong!

* *

Revelation 12:9
The great dragon was hurled down---that ancient serpent
called the devil, or Satan, who leads the whole world astray.
He was hurled to the earth, and his angels with him.

* *

Victorious

The devil drags up all my shame,
But God says, "Let it go!
I sent my Son to take that blame
Two-thousand years ago."

The devil says "You'll never change,"
But God tells me I can;
For Christ came here to rearrange
Old Satan's evil plan.

When Christ cut off the serpent's head
By dying on the cross,
I should have been the one instead
To suffer all that loss.

Yet Jesus gave his life for me
And rose again to say
That He had set us sinners free,
And Satan holds no sway.

* *

Colossians 2:13-15

When you were dead in your sins and in the uncircumcision of your sinful nature, God made you alive with Christ. He forgave us all our sins, having canceled the written code, with its regulations, that was against us and that stood opposed to us; he took it away, nailing it to the cross. And having disarmed the powers and authorities, he made a public spectacle of them, triumphing over them by the cross.

* *

Did Satan Want Jesus on That Cross?

When Christ prayed in the garden
And struggled with despair
And wondered if a pardon
He might be given there,
I wonder if the devil
Thought he had won it all?
Did he begin to revel,
Not sensing his downfall?
Did he think that this world could
Entomb Christ in a cave?
Did Satan think that Christ would
Stay buried in that grave?
Did he not know of God's plan
And what Christ came to do;
That He built a bridge to span
From God to me and you?
I guess old Satan surmised
That death had closed the door,
And he must have been surprised
When Jesus lived once more.

* *

Luke 24:2-8
*They found the stone rolled away from the tomb, but when they
entered, they did not find the body of the Lord Jesus. While they were
wondering about this, suddenly two men in clothes that gleamed like
lightning stood beside them. In their fright the women bowed down
with their faces to the ground, but the men said to them, "Why do
you look for the living among the dead? He is not here; he has risen!
Remember how he told you, while he was still with you in Galilee:*

*'The Son of Man must be delivered into the hands of
sinful men, be crucified and on the third day be raised
again.' " Then they remembered his words.*

* *

Yes, Satan Is Real

I have a rooster that we raised from a tiny chick. He has grown to become a beautiful creature, but believe me when I say that his beauty is only feather deep. He is a good keeper of his flock, and guards them jealously. He is cocky and struts around as proudly as the peacocks in the pen next to his. Oh, he thinks so very highly of himself.

When I am around him, he watches me closely, and, as soon as I turn my back to him, he attacks me with great vengeance. I still have a spot on my leg from his ambush several months ago, and it may never go away completely. Some people ask me why he is still alive after all the damage he has done and will probably continue to do. I have a good reason for letting that rooster live.

Every time I look at him I am reminded that the real Satan is forever trying to attack God's people. He is sneaky and fights "dirty". He is relentless. He is jealous of everything that God has, and he wants it all for himself. He knows that he is not as powerful as he would like for us to think he is, and that causes him to be extremely angry about the way things are. Satan can appear to be a beautiful creature also. He uses his appearance to catch us unaware of the danger he brings.

When I see our rooster Satan, I am always reminded that I must be constantly on my guard against the real Satan. I must resist the temptations that he sends my way. I must pray every day for God's hedge of protection around my loved ones and me. I must put on the full armor of God at all times to protect against the fiery darts of his demons.

So, that rooster is a reminder that I must always be aware that Satan is real. It is certainly true that whatever Satan plans for my harm, my God plans for my good...even if it involves using a rooster.

****

2 Corinthians 11:14
And no wonder, for Satan masquerades as an angel of light.

****

Proverbs 22:3
The prudent see danger and take refuge, but the
simple keep going and pay the penalty.

Satan the Rooster

I have a rooster named Satan, for he is sneaky and sly.
He waits to attack
'Til I turn my back,
Then straight toward my body he'll fly.

He has some hens in his harem who blindly follow his lead.
Like demons in hell
Their souls they would sell
For a little chicken feed.

That rooster struts around proudly, thinking that he is a king.
His head is held high;
He'll kill me, or try,
With his beak or claws or wing.

So, I have learned to be watchful; I am always on my guard.
One day he will be
Called "Dumplings" by me
And no longer in my yard.

* *

1 Peter 5:8-9
*Be alert and of sober mind. Your enemy the devil prowls around like
a roaring lion looking for someone to devour. Resist him, standing
firm in the faith, because you know that the family of believers
throughout the world is undergoing the same kind of sufferings.*

* *

Satan Went to Church

Old Satan went to church one day
 And sat on the back pew.
He did not have too much to say
 To those within his view.
He watched as people took a seat
 With smiles made out of stone.
No one stopped to "meet and greet";
 Their eyes were on their phone.
The pastor's words were cold and dry
 And carefully chosen.
Why should he preach, or even try,
 To hearts that seemed frozen?
He dared not mention certain things
 The Bible says are wrong.
If he offends with words that sting,
 He won't be there for long.
Church had become a ritual,
 The same thing every week.
It seemed to be habitual
 To those who came to seek.
The hymns were sung as if by rote;
 No hands were raised in praise.
The prayers to God were so remote
 They were lost in a haze.
No plans were made to reach the lost
 Or visit those in prison,
Or tell the world how much it cost
 Our Lord who has risen.

There was no mention of a plan
 To help those with afflictions,
And many people wished to ban
 Those struggling with addictions.
It seemed like an eternity

'Til time was up at last.
The congregation all broke free
And scurried out so fast.

But old Satan did no hurry;
He took his time instead.
He no longer had to worry
Because that church was dead.

* *

Revelation 3:1(b)
*These are the words of him who holds the seven spirits
of God and the seven stars. I know your deeds; you have
a reputation of being alive, but you are dead.*

* *

Something Right

I must be doing something right,
For Satan fights me day and night.
He sends his demons to torment
And tries to make me discontent.
It is annoying, I'll admit;
It makes me want to pitch a fit.
He knows my very weakest parts
And aims for them with fiery darts.
He hurts my friends and family
And uses them to get to me.
When I feel things are going well,
He rages from the pits of hell.
My prayers to God make Satan cringe,
For he wants every soul to singe.
Satan knows I am saved by grace,
And he is doomed to lose this race.
Still, he will do all that he can
To carry out his evil plan.
When Satan tries to ruin my day,
I simply stop to kneel and pray.
I can ignore all Satan's lies
If my life's pleasing in God's eyes.

* *

Ephesians 4:27
And do not give the devil a foothold.

James 4:7
*Submit yourselves, then, to God. Resist the
devil, and he will flee from you.*

* *

Then Sings My Soul

Psalm 40:3(a)
He put a new song in my mouth,
a hymn of praise to our God.

Blessings

Verse 1
I have a box in heaven filled with blessings just for me.
God placed them there long ago, for He knew I was to be.
So many days they lay there---all my blessings undisturbed.
All I had to do was ask, for it says so in His Word.

Verse 2
So many of my blessings have been stored there much too long.
I could have used those blessings when my life was going wrong.
I did not stop to ask you to please send some down to earth,
But now, Lord, I realize just how much each blessing's worth.

Chorus
Lord, I now claim my blessings---many more than just a few.
Please pour them out upon me, for I know your Word is true.
Remove the lid and reach inside, Lord, I can scarcely wait.
Please let my one last blessing carry me to Heaven's gate.

Verse 3
Lord, I don't want to leave here with some blessings left unused.
For when I stand before you, I don't want to be accused
Of wasting any blessings that you stored up just for me.
You knew I would face troubles and would need them desperately.

Verse 4
Each morning when I wake, Lord, I will pray for you to send
Another daily ration of blessings with no end.
But when my time is over and my days on earth are through,
Lord, please let my last blessing take me safely home to you.

REPEAT THE CHORUS.

Was It Easy for Him

Lord, I don't understand
Why this load fell on me
I am broken and worn;
Your plan I just can't see.
I have done what I could
To follow your commands,
And I know that my life
Is always in your hands.
But, Lord, it is too hard;
I just cannot go on.
I have bruises and scars
As someone cast a stone.
Lord, I just don't deserve
To feel such agony.
Oh, have mercy, my God;
Remove this thorn from me.

Was it easy for Him
To walk up Calvary's hill?
Was it easy for Him
To do his Father's will?
Was it easy for God
To watch as his Son died?
Was it easy to see
As the spear pierced his side?
Was it easy to know
Some would reject his name?
Was it easy to beat
Satan at his own game?

Jesus suffered and bled
In all that He went through,
So stay faithful, my child,
When it's not easy for you...

Not always easy for you...
He's worth the cost to you.

Then I Felt the Blood

Verse 1

I had lived my life for no one but me,
But I was never satisfied.
I thought I knew best; I thought I was free,
But something was missing inside.
This world called to me; I answered its call,
And Satan took over from there.
I knew I was headed for a big fall,
But I was too stubborn to care.

Verse 2

I refused to see destruction ahead;
I veered from the right to the left.
I felt so secure, and I knew no dread,
Thinking only just of myself.
My heart was so hard it could no longer feel,
And I had no desire to change.
This world offered me such a tempting deal,
And any way else would seem strange.

Verse 3

As days turned to years and life passed on by,
I still had a hunger inside.
From deep down within, I heard a small sigh;
It's something I cannot describe.
Someone shared God's Word, and then I could see
The shame and reproach that I wore.
That space that was void so deep within me
Was barren and empty no more.

Chorus
Then I felt the blood flowing over me
Washing my sins away for all eternity.
Jesus shed his blood so unselfishly.
It was the only way to set this sinner free.

I Will Get You Back

Two little boys, though they were best friends, would sometimes disagree.
This one was right---no that one was---they needed a referee.
One was angry enough to spit;
The other one would pitch a fit.
Then came a threat of dire attack:
You just wait! I will get you back!

A man and wife, after many years, decided to part ways.
He was stubborn---she was so hurt---they had fought for many days,
And neither of them would give in.
It seemed there was no way to win.
Their marriage was so out of whack;
Was there no way to get it back?

Sometimes this world, though it's beautiful, can show an ugly face.
Some are homeless---others hungry---and some feel so out of place.
Crime runs rampant everywhere.
Sometimes it seems we just don't care.
We lose our way and get off track,
But with God's help, we can get back.

When Christ came to this earth below,
And He agreed to suffer so,
God could not stand to let us go
Although our sins were deep and black.
Though Satan tried his level best
To claim us as Hell's special guests,
He was defeated in his quest
When Jesus came to get us back.

John 1:14

The Word became flesh and made his dwelling among us.
We have seen his glory, the glory of the one and only Son,
who came from the Father, full of grace and truth.

I'm Here, Lord

I'm here, Lord, and I'm waiting to hear what you will say.
I'm here, and I am willing to follow you each day.
I can feel your presence, so I need now to be still
And listen for your sweet voice so I can know your will.

I'm here, Lord, in my weakness, just a human so small;
I don't deserve your mercy, yet you died for us all.
I bow down before you, Lord, so amazed by your grace.
I'm here, Lord, please illumine me with light from your face.

I'm here, Lord, I am here! There is no more to be said.
You're always here for me; you're my water; you're my bread.
I'm here, Lord, to worship. I will praise your Holy Name.
I'm here, Lord, you have touched me. I'll never be the same.

I'm here, Lord, come and fill me; let my cup overflow.
I'm here, Lord, can't you feel how my heart yearns for you so?
Your Spirit now controls me, and I have been set free.
Like Isaiah I am pleading, "Here am I, Lord! Send me!"

I am here, Lord, send me!

* *

Isaiah 6:8
Also I heard the voice of the Lord saying, Whom shall I send,
and who will go for us? Then said I, Here am I; send me.

* *

Prayer

VERSE 1

God tells us that we should not fear in this old world of sin,
Though some have tried to change our world into a serpent's den.
God made a perfect home for man, but we weren't satisfied.
Christ came to pay for our mistakes, and on the cross He died.

VERSE 2

God knew that mankind just could not face this world's fears alone,
So, He provided all our friends for us to lean upon.
When Satan tries to make us fear whatever lies ahead,
Our loved ones lift us up with prayers, and faith replaces dread.

CHORUS

Though I may often falter, and I begin to fear
As life comes crashing on me, and Satan's lurking near,
Sometimes in life's dark moments, God's plan I cannot see.
It's in those darkest moments that someone prays for me.

VERSE 3

In my very darkest hour, as fear came creeping in,
My body felt so paralyzed, I felt I could not win
That battle there before me which I was forced to fight.
I felt that I was lost somewhere out in the darkest night.

VERSE 4

Why is it that our darkest times must take us by surprise
As our world seems to fall apart right there before our eyes?
Some trials seem to be much more than we think we can face;
But we are lifted up to God, and we're saved by His grace.

CHORUS

See What He's Done

VERSE 1:
As I stepped out this morning into a brand new day,
I noticed how God's sunshine chased darkness all away.
For just one tiny moment, my entire world stood still,
As all of Heaven's glory just gave my soul a thrill.
I could not help but know that God made this day for me;
He planned it many years ago through eternity.
He saw me standing here today in His scheme of things,
So, He sent this day to me and all the joy it brings.

CHORUS:
See what He's done for me today;
See glory all around.
See how He's led me all the way
To peace and joy I've found.
See just how faithful God has been.
See how He's brought me through.
See what He's done for me, and then
See what He's done for you.

VERSE 2:
As Jesus made His way up a hill called Calvary,
I know He made that journey especially for me.
He did not have to suffer such anguish on that cross.
He could have stayed in Heaven, and my soul would be lost.
But God so loves us all that He sent His only Son,
And He defeated Satan---the victory was won!
All through the years He's watched me and gently shown the way;
Because of grace and mercy, I'm standing here today!

REPEAT CHORUS

Things To Ponder

Proverbs 4:26
Give careful thought to the paths for your
feet and be steadfast in all your ways.

The One or The Nine

I have been healed from sickness severe,
And I have been healed in my spirit.
I've been rescued from dangers so drear,
When I should know not to go near it.

How many times God's blessed me some way,
I surely have no way to know it.
He saved my soul one glorious day!
Does the way I live always show it?

Had I been a leper---one of ten,
Who was healed by our Savior divine,
Would I have said, "Thank you, Lord! Amen!"
Or would I have been one of those nine?

* *

Luke 17:11-19

Now on his way to Jerusalem, Jesus traveled along the border between Samaria and Galilee. As he was going into a village, ten men who had leprosy met him. They stood at a distance and called out in a loud voice, "Jesus, Master, have pity on us!" When he saw them, he said, "Go, show yourselves to the priests." And as they went, they were cleansed. One of them, when he saw he was healed, came back, praising God in a loud voice. He threw himself at Jesus' feet and thanked him---and he was a Samaritan. Jesus asked, "Were not all ten cleansed? Where are the other nine? Was no one found to return and give praise to God except this foreigner?" Then he said to him, "Rise and go; your faith has made you well."

* *

Genesis 1:27
So God created mankind in his own image, in the image of
God he created them; male and female he created them.

The Watchmaker

Each time I see a pocket watch some men like to wear,
I know there was a watchmaker at some time somewhere.
The parts did not fall into place, starting to keep time.
It wasn't just coincidence causing it to chime.
It was not made by accident; designs had been planned.
Each piece was placed so carefully by an unseen hand.
So, it must not be possible, and we can agree,
That watches cannot just appear; that we plainly see.
Now, if watches are created slowly and with care,
By some patient, skillful craftsman working hard somewhere,
Then surely it's not possible that there was no plan
For creation of a wonder as complex as man.
What started in the mind of God, intricate and grand,
Surely led to our creation by our Maker's hand.

* *

Psalm 139:13-16
*For you created my inmost being; you knit me together in
my mother's womb. I praise you because I am fearfully and
wonderfully made; your works are wonderful, I know that full
well. My frame was not hidden from you when I was made in
the secret place. When I was woven together in the depths of the
earth, your eyes saw my unformed body. All the days ordained for
me were written in your book before one of them came to be.*

* *

The Bread of Heaven

How often do I complain
As if I've been wandering for forty years,
So afraid I will remain
Lost and forlorn in a wilderness of tears?

People do not change, it seems.
God promised He will supply my every need,
Even through my shattered dreams.
Yet, thankfulness is often replaced by greed.

Though a thousand things are right,
When one thing goes wrong and life's road gets too rough,
I'm so like an Israelite
For whom the bread of heaven was not enough.

* *

Psalm 105:40
They asked, and he brought them quail; he fed
them well with the bread of heaven.

* *

The Burning Bush

Did I pass by a burning bush today
And not hear it?
I'm sure it had important things to say
Through God's Spirit.
If I encountered it along my way,
Would I fear it?
Or would I stop in awe of its array
And go near it?
Oh, if it said my heart had gone astray,
It would sear it.
I must listen for the voice of Yahweh
And revere it.

* *

Exodus 3:3-4
*So Moses thought, "I will go over and see this strange
sight---why the bush does not burn up."*

*When the LORD saw that he had gone over to look, God
called to him from within the bush, "Moses! Moses!"*

And Moses said, "Here I am."

* *

The Widow's Mite

Some people give a large amount
And make a big production
To show they own a large account,
But it's just an obstruction.
If giving is an act to earn
Some respect you think is due,
Then strike a match and let it burn
For all the good it does you.
God doesn't look at dollar signs;
He's not concerned with flow charts.
He's not obsessed with bottom lines;
He just counts what's in our hearts.
Each one of us should strive to be
Like the widow with her mite,
And no one else should ever see
When we give God what is right.
We must not ever brag or boast
When we give to God above.
To Him the one who gives the most
Is the one who gives with love.

* *

Mark 12:41-44

*Jesus sat down opposite the place where the offerings were put
and watched the crowd putting their money into the temple
treasury. Many rich people threw in large amounts. But a poor
widow came and put in two very small copper coins, worth only
a fraction of a penny. Calling his disciples to him, Jesus said, "I
tell you the truth, this poor widow has put more into the treasury
than all the others. They all gave out of their wealth; but she,
out of her poverty, put in everything---all she had to live on."*

* *

The Road to Emmaus

How many times have I walked the Emmaus Road
And failed to see
That He walked with me?
How many times has Jesus Christ carried my load
When I would fall
And He took it all?
How many times has my Savior wanted to speak
About my day,
But I walked away?
How many times has Christ come to search and to seek
When I was lost
And He paid the cost?
How many times did I not recognize His face
When we would meet
Along this world's street?
How many times have I taken for granted His grace
When He came to die
For one such as I?
How many times have my actions brought Him to tears
When I would sin
Again and again?
How many times have I given in to my fears
When I should just
Believe and trust?
How many times must Jesus keep on forgiving
Each time I fail
To drink from His well?
How long will it be 'til in Heaven I'm living
Where I will be
As faithful as He?

* *

Luke 24:13-35
On the Road to Emmaus

* *

The Valley of Dry Bones

From time to time
   I think we all walk through
      The valley of dry bones.
I know that I'm
   In need of someone who
      Will hear my moans and groans.

An empty shell
   Is how I used to feel
      Until God breathed on me.
And Then I fell
   And God taught me to kneel.
      He set my dry bones free.

When once my life
   Was falling all apart
      He made me all brand new.
He took my strife
   And filled my empty heart.
      He'll do the same for you.

* *

Ezekiel 37:1-6

The hand of the LORD was upon me, and he brought me out by the Spirit of the LORD and set me in the middle of a valley; it was full of bones. He led me back and forth among them, and I saw a great many bones on the floor of the valley, bones that were very dry. He asked me, "Son of man, can these bones live?" I said, "O Sovereign LORD, you alone know." Then he said to me, "Prophesy to these bones and say to them, 'Dry bones, hear the word of the LORD! This is what the Sovereign LORD says to these bones: I will make breath enter you, and you will come to life. I will attach tendons to you and make flesh come upon you and cover you with skin; I will put breath in you, and you will come to life. Then you will know that I am the LORD.'"

* *

A Thirsty Land

We have all been thirsty when there was no drought,
When life-giving water was dammed up by doubt.
Perhaps we were thirsty by our own design;
When each offer was made, we would choose to decline.
Living water is free with just a request;
It provides for our souls such sweet peace and rest.
When we find our water, we should go and share
With those who are thirsty and burdened with care.
Each Christian is part of God's life-giving church,
And we must help others continue their search.
So many around us are dying of thirst
And feel that their lives are forevermore cursed.
Their soul tanks are empty; they sputter and gasp,
With life-giving water so near to their grasp.
Once we have discovered that life-giving well,
Then we've been commissioned to go out and tell
The many lost travelers we meet on our way
That Christ is the water they need every day.
Yet, so many people continue to die
And refuse the water that they pass on by.

* *

Isaiah 32:2
Each man will be like a shelter from the wind and a
refuge from the storm, like streams of water in the desert
and the shadow of a great rock in a thirsty land.

Jeremiah 2:13
My people have committed two sins: They have forsaken
me, the spring of living water, and have dug their own
cisterns, broken cisterns that cannot hold water.

Revelation 21:6
""It is done. I am the Alpha and the Omega, the Beginning
and the End. To him who is thirsty I will give to drink
without cost from the spring of the water of life."

* *

Back to Egypt

When things go wrong, as they so often do,
And tears start to flow,
I wonder how I'll ever make it through,
And I want to go
Back to Egypt.

When times are hard, as they so often are,
Why do I ask, "Why?"
Why do I count each disappointing scar
And desire to fly
Back to Egypt?

And when it seems God has forsaken me,
And I start to doubt,
Why don't I trust instead of constantly
Planning a new route
Back to Egypt?

When nerves are frayed and all my peace of mind
Tumbles from my grip,
I once again start hoping I can find
Some way for a trip
Back to Egypt.

God led me from my wilderness of sin
And heard me complain.
Please show me, Lord, just where I could have been
So I won't remain
Back in Egypt.

Barabbas

I wonder what happened to Barabbas
after he was set free?
Did he make the best of his second chance
or waste it selfishly?
Maybe he went back to his life of crime
and returned to prison,
Or perhaps he gave his life to the One
he knew had arisen.
I like to think that he changed his life and
became a better man.
I hate to think Barabbas ended up
right back where he began.
For like Barabbas, we all stand guilty
Of many debts we owe;
And like Barabbas, someone took our place
so many years ago.
How will we use our second chance in life
since we have been set free?
Will we make Him sad or make Him glad
that He died for you and me?

* *

Mark 15:7-13

*A man called Barabbas was in prison with the insurrectionists who
had committed murder in the uprising. The crowd came up and asked
Pilate to do for them what he usually did. "Do you want me to release
to you the king of the Jews?" asked Pilate, knowing it was out of envy
that the chief priests had handed Jesus over to him. But the chief
priests stirred up the crowd to have Pilate release Barabbas instead.
"What shall I do, then, with the one you call the king of the
Jews?" Pilate asked them. "Crucify him!" they shouted.*

* *

The Middle Lane

I do not like to drive
Along an interstate.
I try to stay alive
And pray it's not my fate
To end up in a heap
Of metal, grit, and glass;
So, I just try to keep
My right foot on the gas.
I do not like to merge
Into a busy lane.
As big semis converge,
It makes me feel insane.
Then suddenly I see
There are three lanes ahead.
The middle lane's for me,
So I drive there instead.
For God knew I would need
A place to calm my nerves
Where I could slow my speed
While traveling 'round the curves.
It makes me stop and think
About a middle man
And of a precious link
That helps us all to span
The gulf from "sin" to "saved"
That we all hope to cross,
For we are born enslaved
And doomed to suffer loss.
But like that middle lane
That helps us on our quest,
Through Christ we can obtain
Our share of Heaven's best.
Now as I travel through
This "testing ground" of life

And search for what is true
Amid turmoil and strife,
I've found a way to solve
My soul's inmost riddle;
My life must now revolve
'Round Him in the middle.

* *

Luke 24:36
While they were still talking about this, Jesus himself stood
among them and said to them, "Peace be with you."

* *

Cafeteria Religion

Some people seem to look at church much as a huge buffet.
They seem to think it's all their choice to choose things their own way.
Hey want the things that suit their taste, like love and understanding.
But they don't want to take the things that seem to be demanding.
Some choose to just sit back and wait while others do the cooking,
And when there's work that must be done, they're the ones just looking.
They talk about humility with just a dash of pride.
They heap on mounds of pampering with envy on the side.
They talk about their daily bread, but do not trust it much.
When they consume the Word of God, they only want a touch.
They want someone to fill their plates but don't tip the waiter.
They seem to think that every church is just there to cater.
Cafeteria religion is not how it should be.
We must let God serve our portions, accepting thankfully.

* *

2 Timothy 2:15
Do your best to present yourself to God as one
approved, a worker who does not need to be ashamed
and who correctly handles the word of truth.

* *

Weeding the Garden

Some flowers bloom a little while and then just fade away.
Some hide a while and then return to bloom another day.
Still others may hang on for years with deeply planted roots,
And year by year continue to put out some fresh new shoots.
So many flowers, as we know, make up a nice bouquet;
But they don't last once they've been cut, and they will soon decay.
For once removed from their life force, they simply can't survive.
They're disconnected from the source that once kept them alive.
Yet, some strong plants, before they die, produce some fertile seeds
And leave behind another crop to carry on their deeds.
Some Christians seem so much like those many kinds of flowers.
Some keep their faith for lifelong years...others just for hours.
Some sow their seeds on fertile ground while some sow none at all.
Some seem so careless with their seeds, not caring where they fall.
As Christians we should strive to bloom until this life is gone,
And we should leave some strong fresh seeds prepared to carry on.
One day it will be much too late to beg for a pardon,
For God will throw away the tares when He weeds His garden.

* *

Matthew 13:27-30

*"The owner's servants came to him and said, 'Sir, didn't you sow
good seed in your field? Where then did the weeds come from?'
"' An enemy did this,' he replied.
"The servants asked him, 'Do you want us to go and pull them up?'
"'No,' he answered, 'because while you are pulling the weeds,
you may uproot the wheat with them. Let both grow together
until the harvest. At that time I will tell the harvesters: First
collect the weeds and tie them in bundles to be burned;
then gather the wheat and bring it into my barn.'"*

* *

The Grouch

I have complained and I have whined
As on fine food I sat and dined.
I have grumbled about a storm
While wearing clothes that kept me warm.
That parking space was much too far,
But from my home I drove my car.
My glasses don't fit me just right,
But I have eyes that still have sight.
Sometimes my life's a tragedy,
But I have friends who pray for me.
Some days I seem to get no rest,
But why complain when I'm so blessed?

* *

Colossians 3:15
Let the peace of Christ rule in your hearts, since as members
of one body you were called to peace. And be thankful.

1 Thessalonians 5:16-18
Rejoice always, pray continually, give thanks in all circumstances,
for this is God's will for you in Christ Jesus.

* *

The Fool

"There is no God," I've heard some say,
And I wonder if they are blind.
How can they think and speak that way,
For He is so easy to find.
He's in a child's sweet newborn cries
And in sunshine and fresh, cool rain.
He paints color in open skies;
He's our comfort when we're in pain.
Our God is here when things go right,
And he is here when life seems wrong.
In darkest times His love is bright.
When we are weak, he makes us strong.
His voice is heard when robins sing
And in laughter as children play.
In fall, winter, summer and spring,
His creation is on display.
It's obvious that God is real;
If we just look, there is no doubt.
Before His throne one day we'll kneel
When we hear His triumphant shout.

* *

Psalm 14:1(a)
The fool says in his heart, "There is no God."

* *

Another Thought from the Laundromat

I have made many new friends at various laundromats as my husband and I have traveled to many places during his years as a pipeline inspector. In a small Texas town, I enjoyed talking to another pipeline wife. During one of our conversations, she mentioned that her husband had read some of my first book, *I Think I Heard A Rooster Crow*. She had told him that she was very surprised that he would be interested in that kind of book since he never seemed to care much about "religion" or God. He asked her, "Don't you think I talk to God?" She replied, "Well, actually, no." He asked, "What do you think I do when I shut myself up in the bathroom for an hour or so with my can of beer, my cigarette, and some reading material?" She told him that she assumed that he was just reading. He informed her that he used that time to talk to God and that he still had the same can of beer in his hand when he came out that he had when he went in. They have been married for several years, but this was good news for her. She told me that she knows a day will come when he will set that can of beer aside, but for the time being it is enough for him to talk to God.

That made us both realize that we all have undesirable habits that God knows all about, but He loves us anyway. Drinking beer is not necessarily a bad thing, as long as it is done in moderation; but that is true about all things. Any action can be taken to excess and become an undesirable trait. We all have some of those actions in our lives, but that does not separate us from God. Not one of us goes to Him with empty, sin-free hands.

* *

1 John 1:8
If we claim to be without sin, we deceive
ourselves and the truth is not in us.

* *

Cigarettes and Beer

I was surprised when my friend said, in joy or tribulation,
That he could sit and talk to God and have a conversation.

His right hand held a cigarette; his left, a can of beer.
Somehow, I never pictured God in such an atmosphere.

He told me how they shared his hurts, his problems and his fears.
He said that often they would laugh and sometimes shed some tears.

He knows one day he'll find the strength to set that can aside,
But until then he's sure his God will take it all in stride.

Not one of us has empty hands when we come to His throne.
We take to God our failures and all the sins we own.

We all have faults and weaknesses, yet God is always near;
Yes, even when we come to Him with cigarettes and beer.

* *

Matthew 9:10-13

While Jesus was having dinner at Matthew's house, many tax collectors and "sinners" came and ate with him and his disciples. When the Pharisees saw this, they asked his disciples, "Why does your teacher eat with tax collectors and 'sinners'?" On hearing this, Jesus said, "It is not the healthy who need a doctor, but the sick. But go and learn what this means: 'I desire mercy, not sacrifice.' For I have not come to call the righteous, but sinners."

* *

Pennies

There's a thought I dearly love
That a penny on the ground
Means that someone up above
Really wants it to be found.
It's sent as a reminder
To a loved one here below
As a message to the "finder"
That love never does let go.
I wish we could find a way ·
For us people here on earth
To reach those who could not stay
Just to let them know their worth.
All the pennies we would cast
Would pile up on Heaven's street.
We would send enough to last
'Til our journey here's complete.
Each penny would let them know
Just how many times each day
They are thought of here below
'Cause love never goes away.
So, when we stop and treasure
Every penny that we find,
We'll feel love without measure
For us loved ones left behind.

* *

1 Thessalonians 3:9
How can we thank God enough for you in return for all the
joy we have in the presence of our God because of you?

* *

Doubting Thomas

I think that, at one time or another,
We all have felt Thomas was our brother.
Doubts arise when we cannot understand,
And Satan tries to get the upper hand.
It seems that we are waiting for a sign;
We want to see the water turned to wine.
We want to see the lame get up and walk.
We want to hear the mute begin to talk.
We want to see the dead man rise once more.
We want to see Christ walk through a locked door.
We want to see His hands and feel His side.
We want to see the Heavens open wide.
Times have not changed from how it was back then.
This world is filled with frightened, doubting men.
We're like the blind man who refused to see,
For miracles abound for you and me.
God asks us to believe in things unseen,
And from His love let nothing come between.
If we just look, we soon will realize
His miracles are right before our eyes.

The Belly of That Whale

(The Book of Jonah)

I did it again...
Put myself right in
The belly of that whale.
God told me to go;
But I did not show,
So now I'm in that whale.
It seems I don't learn,
So, God must get stern
And put me in that whale.
While I'm in "time out,"
I sit there and pout
Once more inside that whale.
I've no one to blame
But me and my shame
While sitting in that whale.
I cry and I yell
Inside of that cell
In that jail in that whale.
I pray and I shout,
"Lord, please let me out!"
While locked up in that whale.
I've had time to think
As I sit and stink
Inside that smelly whale.
At last I can see
How God must see me
Sitting inside that whale.
When He says, "Obey,"
I'll answer, "Okay,"
And stay out of that whale!

* *

John 20:24-29

Now Thomas (called Didymus), one of the Twelve, was not with
the disciples when Jesus came. So the other disciples told him,
"We have seen the Lord!" But he said to them, "Unless I see
the nail marks in his hands and put my finger where the nails
were, and put my hand into his side, I will not believe it."
A week later his disciples were in the house again, and Thomas
was with them. Though the doors were locked, Jesus came and
stood among them and said, "Peace be with you!" Then he said
to Thomas, "Put your finger here; see my hands. Reach out your
hand and put it into my side. Stop doubting and believe."
Thomas said to him, "My Lord and my God!"
Then Jesus told him, "Because you have seen me, you have believed;
blessed are those who have not seen and yet have believed."

* *

The Cross Beside the Road

When I see a cross beside a road,
I know that someone loved and lost.
There's an empty space in some abode
That can't be filled at any cost.
Someone remembers throughout each day
And wishes time could just rewind
To a day before they went away
When life was sweet and fate was kind.
As I feel the love I know they shared
When on this earth their loved one trod,
I pray that someone took time and dared
To tell them of the love of God.
Some things just can't wait until the dawn,
For no one knows the time or place.
It will be too late when they are gone
To tell them of amazing grace.
In that last moment, what did they think,
As they raced toward eternity?
We can leave this world as our eyes blink.
Be ready, Friend, our Lord to see.

* *

James 4:14
Why, you do not even know what will happen tomorrow. What is your
life? You are a mist that appears for a little while and then vanishes.

* *

162

When He Speaks

James 1:22
Do not merely listen to the word, and so
deceive yourselves. Do what it says.

God Said

God said, "We need some company," as He gazed all around.
"I'd like someone to talk to me and make a joyful sound."
God said, "I'll be so good to them and give them everything.
I'll make some 'her' and make some 'him' and I will be their King."
God said, "All I ask in return is that they love me, too.
I'll teach them well, and they will learn exactly what to do."
God said, "I'll give them all free will, for they must have a choice.
I'll give each one a special skill, and each one can rejoice.

So God completed his great plan and said that it was good.
He felt such a great love for man that He walked where they stood,
But God had given man free rein, and soon sin slithered in.
Adam and Eve, Abel and Cain, and we who are their kin
Now owed a debt we could not pay no matter how we tried.
So we still try to run away and find some place to hide.

God said, "I have a heavy heart, and it is filled with grief.
Now I will cause man to depart, though his stay has been brief."
God said, "But there's one righteous man who lives upon this earth.
My Noah can fulfill my plan and give mankind new birth."
God said, "I will provide a way to cleanse them of their stain.
I'll send my Son to earth one day to suffer all their pain."

Now each time we see God's rainbow so high up in the sky,
We think of days so long ago and One who had to die;
And though we make the same mistakes that nailed Him on that tree,
God says, "My heart still often breaks, but they belong to me."

* *

Genesis 1:27 - 9:17

* *

Is Our God Speaking?

As the thunder rolls and lightning splits the sky,
Rain covers the earth where once the land was dry.
Floods rush through the towns destroying everything,
And people take flight like birds on the wing.
The stench of decay is constantly reeking.
I pause to wonder if our God is speaking.

The earth shakes and cracks, and the things man has made
Are pitifully weak and begin to cascade.
There is no defense against nature like that;
Where tall buildings stood, all the earth is now flat.
Amid all the noise of crashing and creaking,
I wonder again if our God is speaking.

From high in the sky, comes a roar deep and loud;
A twister erupts from a huge funnel cloud.
Once more man-made things have no strength to engage;
They're tossed like small toys in a child's fit of rage.
While there in the midst of moaning and shrieking,
Thoughts go through my mind, "Is our God speaking?"

As waves start to hit from one more tsunami,
Man's things twist and fold much like origami.
The waters rush in with a powerful force,
And nothing is safe in the path of its course.
As rescue from harm the people are seeking,
I can't help but ask, "Is our God speaking?"

Sometimes we forget or just don't understand
Our whole world can fit in the palm of God's hand.
His patience is long, but when He's had enough,
The lessons He sends can be forceful and tough.
So, when storms of life are flashing and streaking,
Let's stop and listen, for our God is speaking.

****

Isaiah 28:2

See, the Lord has one who is powerful and strong. Like a hailstorm and a destructive wind, like a driving rain and a flooding downpour, he will throw it forcefully to the ground.

****

Speak to the Rock

When God said, "Moses, speak to that rock,"
Was that so very hard to understand?
Perhaps Moses had a mental block
And thought that he should take his staff in hand.
Moses struck that rock for his glory
Instead of trusting God to do His part.
Sometimes my life relives that story
When I refuse to listen with my heart.
When Moses made that bad decision,
The price he had to pay was very dear.
Now often I try to envision
What it costs me when I refuse to hear.
I know for a fact God's plan is best,
So why don't I just do things in His way?
Yet, many times I still fail that test
And find I too have a high price to pay.

* *

Numbers 20:6-12

*Moses and Aaron went from the assembly to the entrance to the Tent
of Meeting and fell facedown, and the glory of the LORD appeared
to them. The LORD said to Moses, "Take the staff, and you and your
brother Aaron gather the assembly together. Speak to that rock before
their eyes and it will pour out its water. You will bring water out of
the rock for the community so they and their livestock can drink."
So Moses took the staff from the LORD'S presence, just as he
commanded him. He and Aaron gathered the assembly together
in front of the rock and Moses said to them, "Listen, you rebels,
must we bring you water out of this rock?" Then Moses raised
his arm and struck the rock twice with his staff. Water gushed
out, and the community and their livestock drank. But the LORD
said to Moses and Aaron, "Because you did not trust in me
enough to honor me as holy in the sight of the Israelites, you
will not bring this community into the land I give them."*

* *

Speak Up

How long will God wait for us to decide
If we are on His or the devil's side?
We say we serve God and try not to sin,
But the ways of the world keep slipping in.
We condone some things that we just should not,
And we fail to fight against Satan's plot.
We make excuses in these modern days
That we must adjust to the world's new ways.
We don't speak right up when we know we should.
We don't testify every time we could.
God says we must choose without much delay
Between earthly sins or living His way.
He hears our answers when we try to stall
Each time we choose to say nothing at all.
God won't just sit by forever and wait,
For He'll be the One deciding our fate.
We can't serve the world and drink from His cup.
Cast out the silence! Arise and speak up!

* *

1 Kings 18:21
*Elijah went before the people and said, "How long will you
waver between two opinions? If the LORD is God, follow him;
but if Baal is God, follow him." But the people said nothing.*

* *

Who Do You Say I Am?

I came across some scripture that I assumed I knew.
At first I skimmed right through it, not thinking it all through.
The verse was so familiar, it did not need much thought;
I knew what it was saying and what its message taught.

As I continued reading, somehow my eyes returned
To that familiar passage and what I should have learned.
How often had I read it, and yet had failed to see
The question Christ asked Peter was also meant for me?

When Christ asks me the question, "Who do you say I am?"
Does He believe my answer, or is my life a sham?
When others view my witness, I wonder if they see
That Jesus is my Savior, and He resides in me?

That scripture made me question some things I say and do
And realize my failures and what I know is true.
The life I live must show proof I am a child of His,
And there should be no doubt that I know who He is!

* *

Matthew 16:13-16
When Jesus came to the region of Caesarea Philippi, he asked
his disciples, "Who do people say the Son of Man is?"
They replied, "Some say John the Baptist; others say Elijah;
and still others, Jeremiah or one of the prophets."
"But what about you?" he asked. "Who do you say I am?"
Simon Peter answered, "You are the Christ, the Son of the living God."

* *

There Is A Time

Psalm 62:8
Trust in him at all times, you
people; pour out your hearts to
him, for God is our refuge.

For A Time Such As This

How important you are, please never dismiss;
Perhaps you were born for a time such as this:

A time when our land can use your prayers
A time when your friends know someone cares
A time when loved ones have gone astray
A time when prayers keep darkness at bay
A time when someone must take a stand
A time when judgment is close at hand
A time when this world can use your light
A time when deceit makes wrong seem right
A time when courage and hope are gone
A time when it's hard to carry on
A time when Satan is on the prowl
A time when most earthly things seem foul
A time when people say God's not real
A time when you prove how all must kneel
A time when every battle seems lost
A time when you fight despite the cost

Yes, you are important, please never dismiss;
Perhaps you were born for a time such as this.

* *

Esther 4:14(b)
And who knows but that you have come to royal
position for such a time as this?"

* *

The Beginning

When Christ said, "It is finished," while hanging on that tree,
For me life was beginning; my soul had been set free.
The debt I owed was so great, I never could repay;
But Jesus said, "Don't worry. It's paid in full today."
It wasn't paid with money...no silver and no gold.
It wasn't paid with jewels that by men could be sold.
My debt had no co-signer, no legal document;
But God had made a promise kept by his Son He sent.
There was nothing of value existing on this earth
That could pay our souls' ransom, until our Savior's birth.
Just one drop of Heaven's blood made all my sins depart
And cleansed my sin-stained body...my mind, my soul, my heart.

* *

John 19:30
When he had received the drink, Jesus said, "It is finished."
With that, he bowed his head and gave up his spirit.

1 Corinthians 6:11
And that is what some of you were. But you were washed,
you were sanctified, you were justified in the name of
the Lord Jesus Christ and by the Spirit of our God.

* *

Gray

I have been blessed to reach an age
    Where my hair has turned gray.
Though some may fight it with great rage,
    I let mine stay this way.
My God has kept me in His hand
    From birth until today.
My life has gone the way He planned,
    Though I have gone astray.
Each time I've failed to follow Him,
    It's led to much regret.
Some consequences have been grim
    And are not finished yet.
He knows that I will make mistakes
    Time and time again.
I hate to think how his heart breaks
    When I give in to sin.
Yet, His forgiveness knows no bounds
    After so many years.
One day when His great trumpet sounds,
    I'll meet Him with no fears.
He has promised to sustain me
    With mercy and with grace.
He's given me His guarantee
    That I shall see His face.

* *

Isaiah 46:4
Even to your old age and gray hairs I am he, I am he
who will sustain you. I have made you and I will carry
you; I will sustain you and I will rescue you.

* *

Then Morning Came

I was once in a place that was filled with light,
With peace, joy, contentment, and everything right.
Then God planted my soul in an earthly womb,
And it was strange and dark in that tiny room.
I lived there for a while, and then morning came,
As I entered a world where nothing's the same.
I did find some good things as I moved along,
In this world sometimes right, but often so wrong.
I found love and kindness in some that I met,
But some circumstances, I try to forget.
I discovered some things I had never known
Like pain, loss, and sorrow and feeling alone.
There were times when my heart was broken and sore,
And I'd plead to my God, "No more! Please, no more!"
Sometimes in life's darkness I stumbled and fell,
And where I might end up I never could tell.
I felt all was hopeless, but then morning came,
And I ran toward the light, though weary and lame.
I'll continue this trip as long as God wills.
I will travel along life's valleys and hills.
I know darkness will come, but so will the light
In this world filled with wrong, but also with right.
For our life is a test to pass or to fail,
And we can choose Heaven, or we can choose hell.
I made my decision, and then morning came.
Now I'm waiting to hear when God calls my name.

* *

Psalm 5:3
In the morning, O LORD, you hear my voice; in the morning
I lay my requests before you and wait in expectation.

2 Peter 1:19
And we have the word of the prophets made more certain, and you
will do well to pay attention to it, as to a light shining in a dark place,
until the day dawns and the morning star rises in your hearts.

* *

Sit and Wait

When Christ asks me to sit and wait for Him,
Why is that so hard for me to do?
Why do I fill my life up to the brim
With things that merely rust and mildew?
Why do I offer thoughts and suggestions
As if He can't handle things alone?
Why do I bother Him with my questions
And ask about things that are unknown?
He really does not need my opinion;
He simply wants me to sit and wait.
I must not trespass on His dominion
As He tries to pray and contemplate.
"Just sit and wait," Christ says. I ask, "How long?"
"As long as it takes," is His reply.
"My child, why must you always be headstrong
And ask me 'how, when, what, where and why?'
I only need to have your faith and trust
Enough to know I'll do what is best.
You have done all you can, and now you must
Just sit and wait. I'll do all the rest."

* *

Matthew 26:36
Then Jesus went with his disciples to a place called Gethsemane,
and he said to them, "Sit here while I go over there and pray."

* *

He Waits

God has not forgotten
To send his Begotten,
For Christ will come again one day.
God's waiting for us all
To answer to his call,
So for a while He will delay.
God has a great desire
To keep us from the fire
That Hell hopes to entrap us in.
God sacrificed his Son
So victory could be won;
Christ alone saves us from our sin.
Each one makes up his mind,
For one day he will find
When Christ comes, it will be too late.
There is no time to waste;
Please run to God with haste.
We don't know how long He will wait.

* *

2 Peter 3:9
The Lord is not slow in keeping his promise, as some
understand slowness. He is patient with you, not wanting
anyone to perish, but everyone to come to repentance.

* *

Waiting

They waited for years, though not sure for whom.
Someone was coming to save them from doom.
A promise was made to men years ago.
Each day they waited for Jesus to show.

At last the day came, as they had expected,
But often while here, He was rejected.
For most of mankind did not realize
That God in the flesh had come in disguise.

Now we are waiting for Him to return.
In the eastern sky, we soon will discern
God's promise fulfilled when Christ comes to claim
Each of His kinsmen and calls us by name!

But just as people in ages long past
Kept on believing 'til He came at last,
We, too, do not know the hour or the day
When He will return to take us away.

Yet, we still believe, as they did back then,
That He's on His way, though we don't know when.
We know He will come, as we watch and wait;
Not one day early; not one moment late!"

Micah 5:2

"But you, Bethlehem Ephrathah, though you are small among the clans of Judah, out of you will come for me one who will be ruler over Israel, whose origins are from of old, from ancient times."

Matthew 24:42, 44

"Therefore keep watch, because you do not know on what day your Lord will come. So you also must be ready, because the Son of Man will come at an hour when you do not expect him."

John 14:3

And if I go and prepare a place for you, I will come back and take you to be with me that you also may be where I am.

One Brick at a Time

Sometimes it seems that our lives fall apart
And turn into a big pile of rubble.
In this world of woe, it seems from the start
That we are faced with nothing but trouble.
Some face more heartaches than some ever know,
And I wonder how they can get through it.
But from one little seed great faith can grow,
And they know God gives them strength to do it.
Just as Nehemiah once built a wall
Though there were many obstacles to climb,
With God's help, when our lives crumble and fall,
We can rebuild them one brick at a time.

* *

Matthew 7:24

*"Therefore everyone who hears these words of mine and
puts them into practice is like a wise man who built his
house on the rock. The rain came down, the streams rose,
and the winds blew and beat against that house; yet it did
not fall, because it had its foundation on the rock."*

* *

Are We There Yet

Most children, when they travel far,
By plane or train or truck or car,
Soon question after a short while
How far they've gone mile after mile.
To them their journey seems so long,
Though they play games or sing a song.
Their patience soon wears very thin
As they must know how far they've been.
Sometimes our journey on this earth,
As we move forward from our birth,
Can seem to be a game we play
While traveling on this earthly clay.
Some roads are rough and some are fun;
We'll travel both before we're done.
With Heaven as our final stop,
We plod on down this world's blacktop;
Then like a child we start to fret
And ask our God, "Are we there yet?"

* *

2 Corinthians 5:1-8

*Now we know that if the earthly tent we live in is destroyed, we
have a building from God, an eternal house in heaven, not built
by human hands. Meanwhile we groan, longing to be clothed
with our heavenly dwelling, because when we are clothed, we will
not be found naked. For while we are in this tent, we groan and
are burdened, because we do not wish to be unclothed but to be
clothed with our heavenly dwelling, so that what is mortal may be
swallowed up by life. Now it is God who has made us for this very
purpose and has given us the Spirit as a deposit, guaranteeing
what is to come. Therefore we are always confident and know that
as long as we are at home in the body we are away from the Lord.
We live by faith, not by sight. We are confident, I say, and would
prefer to be away from the body and at home with the Lord.*

* *

Late Decisions

"You promised!" she said, as she searched for her key.
"You promised you'd go with our children and me."
She'd stuck by his side after years of abuse,
So this Sunday morn, he could find no excuse.
He knew deep inside he did not want to go;
He knew there were things he did not want to know.
"Just this once," he thought, as he put on his clothes.
"I can go this once just for her, I suppose."
The drive seemed too short; he began to feel tense.
What did she expect? This just didn't make sense.
He knew that she prayed for a change in his life
To improve as a dad and honor his wife,
But what did her church have to do with it all?
He knew that their stares would just make him feel small.
They entered the door; he stayed close by her side.
He wished he could find a safe place he could hide.
Some people shook hands; he was led to his seat.
He tried his best to be very discrete.
They stood for a song and then bowed for a prayer,
And still he wondered just why he was there.
He'd never thought much about all this church stuff.
His life had been hard; it had made him be tough.
Now everyone stood as they all sang some song
About how each one has committed some wrong;
How everyone should just bow down on his face
And thank God above for His Amazing Grace.
Then the preacher rose, and he began to speak
Of a man named Christ who was so mild and meek.
He told how this man was God's begotten Son
And how through this Christ the victory had been won;
How Satan was foiled in his malicious plan
To conquer the world and the downfall of man.
As he heard the Word, something began to stir;
With tears in his eyes he looked over at her.

With eyes tightly closed and her head bowed in prayer,
It seemed that a Spirit was hovering there.
He felt a movement way down deep inside;
This was the moment that his heart must decide.
The first step was hard, but he knew not to wait.
Though his sin was deep, it was still not too late.
He fell on his knees at the feet of his God
And confessed his sins down life's road he had trod.
With face washed by tears and his soul washed with blood,
He found salvation; he was saved from sin's flood.
God made a big change in the life of that man.
What we cannot do, we've a Savior who can.

* *

John 5:24

*I tell you the truth, whoever hears my word and believes him
who sent me has eternal life and will not be condemned;
he has crossed over from death to life.*

* *

Time

Time seems to be a thief as I grow older. I once thought that I had time to spare and to wish away, but now I would like to lasso it and hold it back for a while. Time steals our youth, our energy, our independence, and so much more of our personal lives. Most importantly, time steals those we love. So many times we think, "Just a day ago or a week ago or a month ago or a year ago they were here." So many times we wish to go back to the day before they left to have just a few more moments with them.

God allotted us our time on this journey through our earthly lives, and He allotted us the time we spend with those we love. It is not for us to question His plan, and I don't. As each one of us departs for an eternal home, we leave memories behind. It comes to my mind that those memories then take the place of our time. As long as those memories remain in someone's heart, our time here has not run out. Our souls have departed, but our hearts still remain in the hearts of those who love us.

* *

Ecclesiastes 3:1-2
There is a time for everything, and a season
for every activity under heaven:
a time to be born and a time to die,

John 11:25-26
Jesus said to her, "I am the resurrection and the life. He who
believes in me will live, even though he dies; and whoever lives
and believes in me will never die. Do you believe this?"

1 Corinthians 13:13
And now these three remain: faith, hope and love.
But the greatest of these is love.

* *

The Last Time

On earth there is always a last time:
the last time I'll say goodbye
the last time I'll ever cry
the last time I'll lose my way
the last time I'll see this day
the last time I'll suffer pain
the last time I'll feel the rain
the last time I'll shed a tear
the last time I'll see you here.

In Heaven there will be a first time:
the first time I'll see God's face
the first time I'll see that place
the first time I'll feel His touch
the first time I'll laugh so much
the first time His food I'll share
the first time I'll meet you there.
the first time I'll see His throne
the first time I'm really home

And there will never be a last time.

* *

Revelation 7:17
For the Lamb at the center of the throne will be their shepherd; he will lead them to springs of living water. And God will wipe away every tear from their eyes.

Revelation 21:4
He will wipe every tear from their eyes. There will be no more death or mourning or crying or pain, for the old order of things has passed away.

* *

FINISHING STRONG

I have not always run life's race with power
Or made good use of each and every hour
Or shown an attitude that would make Him proud
To claim me as His child from this worldly crowd.

There have been many times when I've let Him down
And caused His beautiful face to wear a frown.
I've probably made Him pause and wonder why
He willingly came into this world to die.

But I know that I'm the reason that He came
To relieve me of my guilt, my sin, my shame;
And though I break his heart continuously,
His heart's desire is to love and rescue me.

He forgives my failures---rights my every wrong;
I may start weak, but with Him I'll finish strong!

* *

Acts 20:24
However, I consider my life worth nothing to me, if only I may
finish the race and complete the task the Lord Jesus has given
me---the task of testifying to the gospel of God's grace.

* *

Because I Lived

When I have breathed my last on earth,
What will the time I've spent be worth?
Was all my bad outweighed by good?
Did I witness each time I could?
Did I forgive wrongs done to me
As Christ forgave on Calvary?
Did I obey the Spirit's call
And give to God my all in all?
Was one soul helped by what I'd said
About Christ's blood so scarlet red?
When life got hard, did I press on
And keep my faith when hope was gone?
Did I help feed some hungry folks
And help carry their heavy yokes?
Did I visit the ones in jail
And tell them how God's love won't fail?
Did I provide for those in need
And strive to plant salvation's seed?
When I arrive at Heaven's gate,
I know that it will be too late
To make up for the things I should
Have done on earth while I still could.
So, at this time my prayer will be
That my God will be pleased with me.
I pray He'll say when life is done,
"Come in, my child, well done...well done."

* *

Matthew 25:21

*"His master replied, 'Well done, good and faithful servant! You
have been faithful with a few things; I will put you in charge of
many things. Come and share your master's happiness!'"*

* *

Special People
And Events

Galatians 5:22-23
But the fruit of the Spirit is love, joy,
peace, forbearance, kindness, goodness,
faithfulness, gentleness and self-control.
Against such things there is no law.

Pipeline Women

I had no intentions of going on the road
To leave the life I knew so far behind.
Now a travel trailer is mainly our abode
In any RV park that we can find.
Those first uncertain days in some new locations
Would make me feel so lonely I could cry.
This world in which we live has many vocations,
But going on the road we had to try.
In time I discovered more women just like me
Who cope with pipeline life from day to day.
We deal with the fact that there is no certainty
Of when the next job comes so far away.
Some travel with their men, while others stay at home
And go to see their mates each time they can.
But always I have found, no matter where I roam,
A woman who supports her workingman.
Now I have discovered, through all the miles we've spanned,
There is no friend quite like a pipeline wife.
We talk and share our hearts, and now I understand,
That each of you is now my friend for life.

* *

Job 31:32
but no stranger had to spend the night in the street,
for my door was always open to the traveler---

* *

Football and Life

When you walk onto that field to face another foe,
Although it is just a game, there are things you must know.
You must fully be prepared before you start to play,
And you must wear battle gear to march into the fray.
You must learn, for your safety, the proper way to hit.
You follow all instructions, or on the bench you'll sit.
There are pads and hard helmets and shoes with sturdy cleats.
You will face some victories and also some defeats,
But whatever the outcome, you'll walk away with pride
Because you have your coaches and teammates by your side.
Our battle with the devil is more than just a game,
But it seems in many ways it is fought much the same.
Ephesians says to put on the full armor of God
So we will be protected wherever we may trod.
With belt of truth 'round our waist, breastplate of righteousness,
Feet fitted with readiness from peace we can profess.
Our shield is made of strong faith as battle cries are heard,
With helmets of salvation and the sword of God's Word.
Our coaches lead us onward, God's Spirit and his Son,
And we all know the outcome; the battle has been won.
But Satan keeps attacking, so we must hold the line,
And follow Christ's instructions, for they are yours and mine.
We are told to love our God with our heart, soul, and mind
And to stand across the gap for hurting ones we find.
We face the darkest forces that Satan can command,
But fitted with God's armor, we have the strength to stand.

* *

Ephesians 6:11-17

Put on the full armor of God so that you can take your stand against the devil's schemes. For our struggle is not against flesh and blood, but against the rulers, against the authorities, against the powers of this dark world and against the spiritual forces of evil in the heavenly realms. Therefore put on the full armor of God, so that when the day of evil comes, you may be able to stand your ground, and after you have done everything, to stand. Stand firm then, with the belt of truth buckled around your waist, with the breastplate of righteousness in place, and with your feet fitted with the readiness that comes from the gospel of peace. In addition to all this, take up the shield of faith, with which you can extinguish all the flaming arrows of the evil one. Take the helmet of salvation and the sword of the Spirit, which is the word of God.

* *

The Oak Grove High School Motto:

"WHATEVER
IT
TAKES"

* *

Colossians 3:23-24
*Whatever you do, work at it with all your heart, as
working for the Lord, not for human masters, since you
know that you will receive an inheritance from the Lord
as a reward. It is the Lord Christ you are serving.*

* *

Friday Night Lights

When thinking about life in a small, southern town in Louisiana, most of us who abide in such places automatically think of football games on Friday nights. Our little community is certainly well-known for that. Our largest high school is very small, but the students throughout the years have excelled in many activities far beyond the size of the school. Football pride has helped to raise spirits and form a bond among the citizens of West Carroll Parish, even when times have been extremely hard and bleak.

On December 8, 1989, the Oak Grove Tigers from Oak Grove High School traveled to New Orleans to play for the state championship in the Super Dome. Most of the citizens in our parish went around singing Fats Domino's big hit "Walking to New Orleans" as they made the journey to support their Tigers. What memories were made in "The Big Easy" that day!

A couple of days before the game, three of us teachers decided to fix up some "goodie bags" for the players and coaches to have on the bus ride to New Orleans. My inspiration from above hit me and sent the words of the following poem. I went to the school library and borrowed a copy of Clement Clarke Moore's poem called "'Twas the Night Before Christmas" so that I could use it as a pattern for my poem. We included a copy of the following poem with each goodie bag and sent them on the bus with the team.

Even though the poem was written two days before the actual game, it was uncanny how the game played out exactly like the poem. It was hard to believe that it had been written before the event. We all shared a magical time as a community, and I believe that God sent those encouraging words to lift us up and bind us together on that journey. There have been other state championship wins since that one, but this one was especially sweet! When the last whistle blew, the score was 28 to 0 in favor of the Oak Grove Tigers. They broke several championship records in that game and lived up to their motto:

"WHATEVER IT TAKES!"

The Night of the Big Game

'Twas the night of the Big Game, when all through the town
Not a person was stirring, they all were Dome bound.
The banners were hung by the students with care,
In hopes that the Tigers soon would be there.
The fans were all singing and cheering with glee
While visions of championships were all they could see.
And Vic in his headphones, and Kent with his pad
Had brainwashed the Tigers to know that "We're BAD!"
When out on the turf there arose such a clatter,
We sprang from our seats to see what was the matter.
Away toward the goal line Earl flew like a flash;
Keith added one point with one great big bash.
The smiles on the faces of our fans all aglow
Gave the sign of a victory to our Tigers below.
Then Jason and Tony broke right through their line
With Chris, Gerald, and Monty blocking behind.
With Jason's great passing so lively and quick,
We knew that Haynesville must feel mighty sick!
Like one mean machine the Tiger team came;
Vic whistled and shouted and called them by name:
Go, Scott and Dean! Fight, Jimmy and Ray!
Let's make them remember they played us today!
Run, Richie and Matt! Hit, David and Kai!
Kick, James! Catch, Josh! Don't let one man by!
As the Haynesville Tornadoes looked on in dismay,
The tough Oak Grove Tigers continued to play.
So up to the Dome-top the screams and cheers flew,
As our own "home-grown" Tigers knew just what to do.
And Robby and Korwin and Marcus and Ben
And Reggie and Frank said, "It's great to win!"
Todd threw up his arms; Fred was jumping around;
And down the field Emmry came with a bound!
Rodney, Clay, and Joey, Trey, Brad, and Paul
Went wild when our Tigers took over the ball!

Gabriel, Decorian, Charlie, Kenny, and Steve
Watched with much pleasure as Haynesville did grieve.

Scot's eyes---how they twinkled! John's eyes---how they shone!
Kenny Herring was thrilled right down to the bone!
The Tigers were drawn like a powerful bow;
Their target was victory; this was THEIR show!
The cameras were rolling to record this great feat.
No one could manage to stay in his seat.
Each face from Oak Grove was sporting a smile.
The Tigers had traveled that last long, hard mile!
We were happy and thrilled; a dream had come true!
The Tigers had done all that they had to do!
With a tear in each eye and a prayer of thanksgiving,
We knew that this day was well worth the living!
The last whistle blew; the victory was complete.
Like one solid body, Oak Grove jumped to its feet!
Our Tigers were tired, but they stood oh so proud!
They had given their best for their own hometown crowd.
The trophy was given and received with great care
As tears of happiness flowed everywhere.
Now we in Oak Grove have one thing to say,
"Look, World, our Tigers are CHAMPS of CLASS A!!!"

* *

James 1:4
Let perseverance finish its work so that you may be
mature and complete, not lacking anything.

* *

ACHILLES

We shared our lives with Achilles for five-and-one-half years. He lived in our home whenever we were at home, and he lived in our travel trailer whenever we were off on a pipeline job. We have been at home for a little over two months now, and it was a joyful time of holiday fun and family until this past Friday. I was at my mother's house in Archibald, and Mike was at home. Achilles came home, and Mike noticed that he had a small scrape on his side. Achilles threw up some food, but that was not unusual for him because he had a very weak stomach, and Mike assumed he had eaten something outside that had made him ill. Achilles went through his usual nightly routine. He climbed into his recliner in the den while Mike watched television. He climbed upon his couch in the bedroom when Mike went to bed. Mike petted him, and Achilles wagged his tail, as usual. The next morning, when Mike got up, Achilles had moved to the floor at the foot of our bed, and he was dead. Mike examined him and discovered that the small scrape on his side was actually a bullet hole---probably a 22-caliber bullet hole. Someone had shot him.

Yes, Achilles was a pit bull, and some people are scared of them. They, like many people, are judged by their appearance instead of their hearts. Usually he stayed around on our land, but perhaps he had rambled off where he should not have been; however, he was wearing a bright orange collar with Mike's name engraved on it and both of our cell phone numbers. A simple telephone call could have been made just asking us to come pick him up and keep him away from wherever he was. Some of our neighbors' dogs wander onto our property from time to time, but we do not shoot them. He was a loving, harmless dog and never threatened anyone. He was a member of our family. He is now buried in our backyard, and we have ordered a stone engraved to mark his resting place.

I am glad that we do not know who shot Achilles. Somehow it seems easier to try to forgive some evil without a face than it would be to forgive evil with a face. I cannot imagine the kind of person who could do such a thing---especially since all of the people around us know that he belonged to us. Mike said that it probably was not a deer hunter because the caliber of the bullet could not have killed a deer. It had to have been someone who carefully and purposely took aim and took a life that was very dear to us. He was dear to everyone in our families.

Achilles was my constant companion whenever we traveled to and from jobs. He rode in my excursion with me while Mike pulled the travel trailer with his truck. One of his greatest pleasures, however, was riding in the back of the truck. Sometimes we went for rides just to please him. Achilles and I took walks three times a day when we were at campsites. We waited for his "daddy" to come home from work, and Mike was always greeted with barks and wet kisses. How I will miss our walks! How we will miss those rides! How Mike will miss his "shadow"! How we will miss the way he always sat or lay on our feet because that was where he felt secure and safe and loved! How we will miss how he would lie as close to us as he could possibly get! How we will miss his big, wet kisses when he would give us "sugar"! How we will miss all of the tricks he did whenever he wanted a treat! How we will miss how he would "talk" to us! How we will miss all of the sad looks and guilt trips he always gave us whenever we went somewhere that he couldn't go! How we will miss the way he greeted us when we returned! How we will miss the way he was afraid to walk across the kitchen floor (or any slick-looking floor anywhere) because he thought he would slip down! How we will miss seeing him curled up in his blue recliner or on his couch! How we will miss his scratch at the door and seeing him sitting there until we told him to come in! How we will miss so many things! How we will miss Achilles!

Men of God

At this point in history, there seems to be
A need for more men of God to help us see
How we all must take a stand for what we know,
And we can't let Satan's team drag us below.

It seems there's a shortage of men who will lead
And honor the name of God in thought and deed.
I know God is counting on His faithful few
To rise up against the foe and remain true.

Man's time here is running out, I do believe,
And we all must do our part before we leave.
We pray and we testify and read His Word,
And then share with all mankind who have not heard.

So, please just keep pressing on, standing for right,
And in this dark sinful world, you'll be God's light.

* *

Philippians 3:14
I press on toward the goal to win the prize for which
God has called me heavenward in Christ Jesus.

* *

Daddy's Girl

When I was young I always was my daddy's little girl.
I learned to dance while balancing on top of his big feet.
I'd hold on tightly to his hands as 'round the room we'd whirl;
Like Fred Astaire and Ginger, this pair no one could beat.

I felt so safe when he was near; I loved those jokes he told.
I followed him most everywhere that he would let me go.
His family was his pride and joy; we were his pot of gold.
He wanted everything for us, and seldom told us, "No."

He lived a life most wonderful and made some friends so dear;
But years will take their toll on man---yet only in this world.
We felt our Savior's presence as his time to go drew near;
He smiled as he walked toward the light of Heaven's gates unfurled.

Now years have passed since he walked here upon this earthly sod.
"I'd love to see him one more time," my lonely heart repeats.
It's been so long since he went home to Heaven and his God;
But when I see him once again, we'll dance on golden streets.

* *

John 14:2-3
Jesus said, "In my Father's house are many rooms; if it were not
so, I would have told you. I am going there to prepare a place
for you. And if I go and prepare a place for you, I will come back
and take you to be with me that you also may be where I am."

* *

Where Do Pastors Come From?

God was busy creating a man;
He had for him a most special plan.
He gave him courage to speak the truth
And loyalty much like that of Ruth.
God made a heart filled up to the brim
With love and compassion sent from Him.
God made that heart both gentle and strong,
For though it might break when things went wrong,
That heart would still praise through every test
The God who placed it in that man's chest.
Much wisdom was poured into his mind
And patience to face each daily grind.
Contentment and joy were placed inside,
Then God made sure they were multiplied,
For this man must know salvation's worth
And not be concerned with riches on earth.
God filled the man with understanding
And strength to stand when times were demanding.
God spoke to him and taught him to pray,
And he soon learned to trust and obey.
God gave him the will to rise and go
To whatever place his God would show.
The man got a call from his Master,
And that's how God made our good pastor.

2 Timothy 4:1-5

In the presence of God and of Christ Jesus, who will judge the living and the dead, and in view of his appearing and his kingdom, I give you this charge: Preach the Word; be prepared in season and out of season; correct, rebuke and encourage---with great patience and careful instruction. For the time will come when men will not put up with sound doctrine. Instead, to suit their own desires, they will gather around them a great number of teachers to say what their itching ears want to hear. They will turn their ears away from the truth and turn aside to myths. But you, keep your head in all situations, endure hardship, do the work of an evangelist, discharge all the duties of your ministry.

We Don't Understand

On the night of December 1, 1995, a tragedy occurred in our small community. A young boy and a young girl lost their lives in an automobile accident. The young boy was the son of one of my best friends. I had known John for all of his fifteen years, six months, and twenty-two days of life. I had watched him grow from a shy little boy into a sweet, handsome young man who loved to kick a football through the goalposts during the Friday night high school games. He was only a freshman in high school, but he was already excelling as a kicker. I can remember seeing him practice out on the football field and at his home when he was barely bigger than the football itself. That dedication to his craft continued until his last day on earth. The last photograph that I took of John was of him kneeling on one knee and holding a football on the other.

John was not only a good athlete and an excellent student. He was also very involved in his church activities and was showing a great concern (even at his young age) for the salvation of his friends. He led by example both on and off the football field. Everyone who knew him knew about his relationship with his God and his Savior.

His mother and I often wonder what John would be doing if he were still with us in this world. We can imagine great things he would have accomplished and a wonderful family he would have. He touched so many lives in a positive way while he was here, and we can't understand why God chose to take him home so soon. Yet, we know that it is not for us to understand at this time. It will all become clear when we are reunited in Heaven, just as so many other grieving parents will one day understand why they had to endure such a loss. Until then, we must just understand that **we do not have to understand;** we must **trust** that God understands.

* *

Romans 8:28
And we know that in all things God works for the good of those
who love him, who have been called according to his purpose.

* *

Our John

We know not why, in God's great plan,
A boy must die---not yet a man.
For fifteen years his gifts we shared;
Now through our tears, we know he cared
About his friends and family.
Our faith depends on bended knee,
As to our God we go for peace;
This road we've trod, but pain won't cease.
We should not ask, but yet we must,
Just why this task was put on us.
Why must we live without our joy?
Why must we give our baby boy?
Lord, you must know we cannot see
Why he did go to be with Thee,
And we had such a little while
To hold and touch our precious child.
We know you love him more than we,
And up above with you he'll be;
But it hurts so to send him there,
To let him go where we can't share
In all the things he'll do for you
Our King of Kings eternity through.
Lord, may I say it is my dream
That John may play on your ball team.

* *

John 5:24
"I tell you the truth, whoever hears my word and believes him
who sent me has eternal life and will not be condemned;
he has crossed over from death to life."

* *

Seventeen Years Later

I thought he was invincible
and would never go away.
It simply wasn't sensible
that he could not always stay.
He always gave such wise advice,
and he told his famous jokes.
He taught us to always be nice
to all the other folks.
His presence helped to ward off fear
when troubles would beset us.
I thought that he would still be here
when Jesus came to get us.
Although I thought he could not die,
God had other plans in store;
But on one thing I can rely...
we'll meet again on Heaven's shore.

* *

1 Thessalonians 4:13-14
Brothers and sisters, we do not want you to be uninformed
about those who sleep in death, so that you do not grieve like
the rest of mankind, who have no hope. For we believe that
Jesus died and rose again, and so we believe that God will
bring with Jesus those who have fallen asleep in him.

* *

My Country

Isaiah 9:6
For to us a child is born, to us a son is given, and the government will be on his shoulders. And he will be called Wonderful Counselor, Mighty God, Everlasting Father, Prince of Peace.

To Stand

The evil in this world gets worse each day,
Yet we must stand.
So many times we don't know what to say,
Yet we must stand.
So much of what we love has gone away,
Yet we must stand.
We've watched our country's morals all decay,
Yet we must stand.
Some people try to tell us sin's okay,
Yet we must stand.
God gives us strength and armor when we pray,
So we can stand.

* *

Ephesians 6:13
Therefore put on the full armor of God, so that when the
day of evil comes, you may be able to stand your ground,
and after you have done everything, to stand.

* *

The Handwriting on the Wall

I love my country and hate to see
The evil that now exists.
What once was called the land of the free
Is held in corruption's fists.
We watch the news as crime multiplies
And hear of much disaster.
Politicians cheat before our eyes;
Greed seems to be their master.
"Something for nothing," many demand,
And government says, "Okay,"
Then takes from every hard-working hand
A great big chunk of our pay.
The news seldom tells things as they are,
And it makes us all suspect
They'll go to extremes, bold and bizarre,
For ones they wish to protect.
Our allies are being pushed away;
Our leaders bow down to foes.
Our soldiers take a cut in their pay,
As animosity grows.
Why do we still judge people we meet
By the color of their skin?
Why do we murder a babe so sweet
Before his life can begin?
Let's pray to our God on bended knee
To not let our country fall.
Do we have to wait until we see
The handwriting on the wall?

Daniel 5:5-6, 17-20, 22-28, 30

Suddenly the fingers of a human hand appeared and wrote on the plaster of the wall, near the lampstand in the royal palace. The king watched the hand as it wrote. His face turned pale and he was so frightened that his legs became weak and his knees were knocking.

Then Daniel answered the king, "You may keep your gifts for yourself and give your rewards to someone else. Nevertheless, I will read the writing for the king and tell him what it means.

"Your Majesty, the Most High God gave your father Nebuchadnezzar sovereignty and greatness and glory and splendor. Because of the high position he gave him, all the nations and peoples of every language dreaded and feared him. Those the king wanted to put to death, he put to death; those he wanted to spare, he spared; those he wanted to promote, he promoted; and those he wanted to humble, he humbled. But when his heart became arrogant and hardened with pride, he was deposed from his royal throne and stripped of his glory.

"But you, Belshazzar, his son, have not humbled yourself, though you knew all this. Instead, you have set yourself up against the Lord of heaven. You had the goblets from his temple brought to you, and you and your nobles, your wives and your concubines drank wine from them. You praised the gods of silver and gold, of bronze, iron, wood and stone, which cannot see or hear or understand. But you did not honor the God who holds in his hand your life and all your ways. Therefore he sent the hand that wrote the inscription.

"This is the inscription that was written:

MENE, MENE, TEKEL, PARSIN

"Here is what these words mean:

Mene: God has numbered the days of your
reign and brought it to an end.

Tekel: You have been weighed on the scales and found wanting.

Peres: Your kingdom is divided and given to the Medes and Persians

That very night Belshazzar, king of the Babylonians, was slain, and Darius the Mede took over the kingdom, at the age of sixty-two.

Standing Watch

(Written in 2014)

As I sit here on our front porch this morning, I feel a sense of peace that I desperately need. So many things in my life seem to be "up in the air" lately, and most of those things are completely out of my control. I do have the assurance that God IS in control, however, so I am relying on that promise. Still, I am human (and a woman) so it is hard to ward off that feeling of uneasiness that I know I should not be feeling. Maybe uneasiness is not the correct word; perhaps it is more a feeling of discontentment, which I must also try to guard against. I must be like the Apostle Paul and be content in every situation, knowing the One who is in charge of my life and who loves me beyond measure.

Once again, the morning news upset me when a family was fighting a school system to have the words "under God" removed from the Pledge of Allegiance at their school. That family did not believe in God and thought it was against their "rights" to have those words included in the pledge. One family could possibly overrule the "rights" of countless other families who DO want those words included. I pray that this time a stand will be made to assure that the rights of us who are Christians will be honored. No child is forced to repeat those words. It is a personal choice, but the "right" thing is to HAVE THAT CHOICE!!!

This may sound a little strange, but those of you who know me know that I have a tendency to be a little strange. I am looking at a concrete statue of a squirrel and a plastic statue of a rabbit that have been standing guard on our front porch for over nineteen years. They look out toward the west as if waiting for something they are expecting to happen at any moment. They are faithful in their watch. How I wish we Christians would be as faithful in our watch as we wait for our Master's return. Our faces should be turned toward the eastern sky everyday as we wait faithfully. How we should be standing up for OUR beliefs instead of sitting back and letting a few lost souls try to push God completely out of our country. I WANT HIM BACK IN FULL FORCE! However, I do not do everything that I should be doing to make sure that He does not leave America. I am not exactly sure what I can do; but I pray for our country, and I try to pray for some of our leaders who are obviously lost. (Sometimes they make me so mad that it is actually hard to pray for them, but God knows that I try.) My heart grieves for our country that was built on a strong belief in God. I know that we believers must outnumber those who do not believe, but we do not seem to be proving that fact. Maybe we need one big revival in a central location like those that Billy Graham presided over. Let us all pray for God to once again have COMPLETE control of America. He hears our earnest prayers. When we come together to pray in agreement, He promises to be there with us and to hear our prayers. I don't believe that He has left our country, but I do believe that He is waiting for His people to say, "Enough!"

* *

Micah 7:7
But as for me, I watch in hope for the LORD, I wait
for God my Savior; my God will hear me.

* *

Heaven Is Crying Today

Heaven is crying today. Heavenly tears are running down my windowpanes. I think maybe God and His angels are weeping for America, as Christ grieved for Jerusalem. *"O Jerusalem, Jerusalem, you who kill the prophets and stone those sent to you, how often I have longed to gather your children together, as a hen gathers her chicks under her wings, but you were not willing! Look, your house is left to you desolate. I tell you, you will not see me again until you say, 'Blessed is he who comes in the name of the Lord.'"* *(Luke 13:34-35)*

In *John 11:35* we read that *"Jesus wept."* That time Christ was weeping in response to the grief expressed by Mary over the death of her brother Lazarus. Even though Jesus knew he would raise Lazarus from the land of the dead, He still expressed His humanity by sharing in their grief. How many times do we make Christ weep as He witnesses our actions and hears our words?

I feel more and more that today Christ is grieving over America much as He grieved over Jerusalem. Christians have stood by and let a few people push God out of our country. I want Him here to stay! *Then he said, "May the Lord not be angry, but let me speak just once more. What if only ten can be found there?"* **(Genesis 18:32)**. Surely there are at least ten righteous people left in America. Let God's people fall to their knees in prayer for His guidance and strength, and then stand up with determination to keep God in America!

I Wonder

I wonder if God turns away and maybe sheds a tear
When He observes the things we say and what we do down here?
I wonder how He feels when we destroy the things He's made,
And we forget that we are free because the price was paid?
I know He's disappointed when He sees our greed and pride
And how ungrateful we have been and how we've often lied.
Perhaps the thought goes through His mind, "Oh, why do I bother?"
How often do we show mankind that He is our Father?
When will His patience just run out, and He says, "It's done"?
How long before we hear a shout and then behold His Son?
How many will be left behind when Jesus comes once more?
How many faithful will He find to take to Heaven's door?
How disappointed God must be when He looks down on man.
What do I say when He asks me, "Do you do all you can?"

* *

Matthew 24:36, 42, 44

*36 " No one knows about that day or hour, not even the
angels in heaven, nor the Son, but only the Father.*

*42 "Therefore keep watch, because you do not
know on what day your Lord will come.*

*44 So you also must be ready, because the Son of Man
will come at an hour when you do not expect him.*

* *

Benghazi

"What difference does it make?" she said,
Though four brave patriots are now dead.
Does she really think that no one cares
As a lonely widow sits and stares
At a photo of her wedding day
And a husband who's now gone away?
Is her heart so hard she can't believe
That they left parents here to grieve
And children now with their fathers gone
Without their guidance to carry on?
Those men had friends and families,
But she chose to ignore their pleas.
They needed help, but none ever showed
To aide them with their heavy load.
Perhaps it might have meant much more
If death had come knocking on her door.

This was written after the 2012 Benghazi attack in which four Americans were killed. Hillary Clinton, as Secretary of State for the United States of America, received much criticism for the way in which she handled that situation.

America in 2012

Sometimes I wonder what our God would have said,
Because it appears we want Satan instead.
We must not remember some things from the past
When men put their faith in the things that won't last.
We should go to His throne on each bended knee,
For it's by His grace we're the land of the free.
Perhaps we've been spoiled just a little too much,
And we have forgotten that we need His touch.
We seem to think that we can make it alone;
So, now we will know how it feels when He's gone.
The majority rules, so He'll step aside;
But with those who do want Him, He'll still abide.
America was the leader of nations;
I think it is one of His best creations.
Our actions today are to Him no surprise;
We're building on sand, like the man so unwise.
We have chosen the path that we want to trod;
I pray America turns back to our God.

* *

Jeremiah 8:12-13
*"Are they ashamed of their loathsome conduct? No, they have
no shame at all; they do not even know how to blush.
So they will fall among the fallen; they will be brought
down when they are punished," says the LORD.
"'I will take away their harvest, declares the LORD.
There will be no grapes on the vine. There will be no
figs on the tree, and their leaves will wither. What I
have given them will be taken from them.'"*

* *

Have We Gone Too Far?

Has our country gone too far to turn back?
Is it too late to ward off sin's attack?
How soon will our Lord's patience just expire
And this whole world be cast into the fire?
Though man may live on water and on bread,
God's Word is how our empty souls are fed.
We must be filled with manna from His Word
And share it with the ones who have not heard.
If all His written words were to be lost,
We'd try to get them back at any cost.
If we wish for our country to survive,
We all must strive to keep His Word alive.

* *

Amos 8:11-12
*"The days are coming," declares the Sovereign Lord, "when I
will send a famine through the land---not a famine of food or a
thirst for water, but a famine of hearing the words of the LORD.
Men will stagger from sea to sea and wander from north to east,
searching for the word of the LORD, but they will not find it."*

* *

New Year 2017

So often when we talk to God, we make a new request,
And we ask for extra blessings to add to all the rest.
It seems we're never satisfied with how things are down here.
We ask that God will take our trials and make them disappear.
We pray for health and wealth and peace for us and others too,
Forgetting that we gain our strength from hard times we go through.
God gave his Son to save us all, and that should be enough;
His grace and mercy's all we need without the other "stuff."
God knows much better than we do our each and every need.
I know sometimes our prayers to Him seem to be filled with greed.
I wonder if He wishes we would change our point of view
And simply kneel and ask our God, "What can we do for you?"

* *

Hebrews 4:16
Let us then approach the throne of grace with confidence, so that we may receive mercy and find grace to help us in our time of need.

* *

Hurting

America, my heart grieves for you
Because of what you are going through.
Once you were held in such high esteem
People traveled here to fulfill their dream
Of a better life for their family
In the land of opportunity.
Our faith in God kept our country strong
Until politicians came along
And ignored the laws that God had made;
They said things were right that He forbade.
We can now kill babies...that's okay;
Their lives don't matter...throw them away.
Marriage no longer follows God's plan;
Now it's two women or man with man.
My Bible tells me that isn't right...
An abomination in God's sight.
Some don't believe, and I realize
They look at this world through different eyes.
God's Word does not mean one thing to them,
And they don't expect judgment from Him.
We are now destroying each other,
Though God tells us to love our brother.
The actions of a few evil men
Are causing a war we just can't win.
Our "men in blue" are under attack;
In an ambush, it's hard to fight back.
Some of our leaders are so corrupt
They seem to want our peace to erupt.
They fill the news with hatred and lies;
And, little by little, freedom dies.
They have a plan to make us disarm
And leave us no protection from harm.
They've sold us out with national debt...
The largest one in our history yet.

The ones who have fought and died for us
Now feel forgotten...not worth the fuss.
All our borders are flung open wide
To welcome our enemies inside.
People we should be able to trust
Betray us for cash, power, and lust.
They're willing to plant a hate-filled seed
To satisfy ambition and greed.
Our country is hurting more and more.
There's only one way we can restore
America, the land of the free;
We must go to God on bended knee.
If you don't agree, that is okay.
I'll keep praying; you do things your way.

* *

Job 31:15
Did not he who made me in the womb make them?
Did not the same one form us both within our mothers?

Romans 1:26-27
Because of this, God gave them over to shameful lusts. Even
their women exchanged natural sexual relations for unnatural
ones. In the same way the men also abandoned natural
relations with women and were inflamed with lust for one
another. Men committed shameful acts with other men, and
received in themselves the due penalty for their error.

2 Chronicles 7:14
If my people, who are called by my name, will humble themselves and
pray and seek my face and turn from their wicked ways, then will I
hear from heaven and will forgive their sin and will heal their land.

* *

He Set Me Free

Isaiah 61:1
The Spirit of the Sovereign Lord is on me,
because the LORD has anointed me to
proclaim good news to the poor. He has
sent me to bind up the brokenhearted,
to proclaim freedom for the captives and
release from darkness for the prisoners.

Dear God

After all the years and all I've done,
You sit and wait for your prodigal son.
Here I come now, I'm running to you.
When I get close, I see you're running, too.
I fall at your feet, but you lift me up.
You call for the calf, my golden cup.
They say I'm not worthy, this sinner I've been;
But thanks to your Son, I've been born again.
Praise the Lord for staying true!
Hey! I think I heard a rooster crow, too.

Written by: Tanner
March 15, 2017

* *

Luke 15:11-32
The Parable of the Lost Son

* *

Drug Court Letter

Our child became a stranger
And stumbled into danger,
Though we tried everything we knew to do.
We always stood behind him;
Sometimes we could not find him.
The more we talked, the more he just withdrew.

Then he was put in drug court,
Where we were given support.
At last we had the help for which we prayed.
We wondered if we'd make it;
At times we could not take it,
But now we thank the good Lord that we stayed.

He's changed back into someone
Who is happy now and fun.
Our grateful hearts go out to all of you.
Each day he's getting better;
With joy I write this letter.
We're getting back the child that we once knew.

* *

2 Corinthians 5:17
Therefore, if anyone is in Christ, the new creation
has come: The old has gone, the new is here!

* *

After Drug Court

We've talked through hours of therapy, and often disagreed.
We've wondered time and time again if ever we'd succeed.
We have sat in countless courtrooms waiting to hear our fate.
We have watched the clock for curfew, striving not to be late.
Many weekends spent in Green Oaks were meant to prove a point.
Obey the rules, don't run away, and NEVER smoke a joint!
The judge just will not hesitate to take away your phone,
And certainly she does not care how much you gripe and groan.
A few days spent in solitude should make one stop and think.
That's not a place to spend a life because of drugs and drink.
Community service helps us to see how some folks live,
And we can receive a blessing when we take time to give.
Through work we learn there is value in paying one's own way
And knowing we have done our best at the end of the day.
It's been a roller coaster ride with many ups and downs.
At first we saw very few smiles and way too many frowns.
We've traveled down a hard, rough road; the journey has been long.
Now we have learned, to make it through, one must be very strong.
I may be wrong, but I believe there is a special hell
For the ones who lead God's children along a drug-filled trail;
And there is a place in Heaven for those who sacrifice
And give their all to help a child to overcome that vice.
Now graduating from drug court is something very fine,
But please say to yourself each day, "From here the choice is mine."

* *

Psalm 119:9-11
How can a young person stay on the path of purity? By
living according to your word. I seek you with all my heart;
do not let me stray from your commands. I have hidden
your word in my heart that I might not sin against you.

* *

A Life of Addiction

There seem to be very few families that have not been hurt by some kind of substance abuse. Those of you who have missed that heartache are most fortunate. I never would have thought that we would ever be faced with a drug or alcohol problem by a member of our family, but we have not escaped that curse. Seeing firsthand the damage that drugs do, not only to the addict but also to everyone who loves him (or her), it makes me extremely angry. So many lives have been lost or destroyed needlessly. That anger branches out in several directions including the addict, the addict's so-called "friends," the people in charge of the law (although I know they are fighting a war that is practically impossible to win), and most of all, I am so very angry at the drug dealers who make and sell the drugs.

Taking a look at *1 Corinthians 8:9 and 12*, we find Paul warning the people.

Verse 9 Be careful, however, that the exercise of your freedom does not become a stumbling block to the weak.

Verse 12 When you sin against your brother in this way and wound their weak conscience, you sin against Christ.

I wonder if the people who make drugs, sell drugs, or get a "cut" from the sale of drugs know or care anything about the *Bible*. Do they not realize the harm they are doing to so many of God's children...the very children for whom He gave his life? Do they not care that Christ also shed his blood for them? I suppose they either don't know or, most likely, just don't care. My anger at them makes it very hard for me to pray for them, although I must. They have caused us and others so much pain that I sometimes think they deserve whatever punishment they get, yet I must pray for their souls and hope they find redemption before it is too late. After all, I also deserve punishment that I will not have to undergo because Jesus took care of that the moment I first trusted in Him.

I know that our loved ones make a choice to do what they

do, at least at first; but then the addiction sets in. That was Satan's plan all along, and he has many helpers. Once they are "hooked," then it leads to more crime such as theft and even murder. What a field day Satan must be having with his drug business! It seems that Christ's workers are becoming fewer while Satan's team is expanding. That is to be expected in these end times.

Another thing that really bothers me is when people tell us that we should just give up on our loved ones because they will never change or amount to much of anything. Yes, we must be careful not to become enablers, but that does not mean that we just "give up." We remember the child who was once so happy and smart. We remember the sweet hugs and the words "I love you." We remember the innocence of the "pre-drug" years. We still look deeply into those beautiful eyes and see a soul that Christ tells us is still worth fighting for. We know that as long as there is life there is still hope. We *BELIEVE* in the miracles that our God can perform.

Some of the following poems in this section were written by people who have fought addictions. I have included their names with their permission, and I hope that you can hear their hearts as you read their words. The poems in this chapter that came from my heart have been hard-earned over several years, as I have seen some of my loved ones struggling with addictions. With God's help, we will all win.

* *

Jeremiah 29:11
"For I know the plans I have for you," declares
the LORD, "plans to prosper you and not to harm
you, plans to give you hope and a future."

* *

Praise from the Prison

As I watch the faces of the women wearing ill-fitting jumpsuits, many thoughts pass through my mind. Most of them have little of this world's wealth; yet, I am amazed as they raise their voices in song and their hands in praise for the things the Lord has done for them. They have heard the truth of salvation and the message of real freedom, and they desire to have it...even from behind prison bars. They are beginning to realize that they are never alone if they call on the name of Jesus.

I see them weep uncontrollably. On many occasions my shoulders have become wet from their tears. I hear them laugh---really laugh--- perhaps for the first time in a long time. I feel their hugs as we greet them and they learn to welcome a small kindness of human contact that wants nothing from them and never condemns them. I listen as they discuss what they have learned from their Bible studies. I begin to see a little self-worth return to their faces.

Sometimes when I watch the women during our prison ministry time with them, I am reminded of Acts 16:25 which states: *"About midnight Paul and Silas were praying and singing hymns to God, and the other prisoners were listening to them."* The presence of God's Holy Spirit is strong in that room; it hovers over us all with a love that is totally unconditional and everlasting. Only God knows just how far the outreach from those women will go. They have started Bible studies in their cells and have learned to pray for one another. When they are released from prison, some of them will become great witnesses for their Savior because they have endured many trials and prevailed. They are captives who have found true freedom behind prison bars.

In this chapter I am including a few poems and articles that were written by two of the women I met during the prison ministry. They are beautiful, intelligent women who just happened to make some wrong choices that led them

232

to that place. Sometimes God will put us in a place where we have the time to be still and know that He is God. If that means time in a prison, then it is worth it if that time leads to salvation.

* *

James 5:13
Is anyone among you in trouble? Let them pray. Is anyone happy? Let them sing songs of praise.

* *

Have You Ever

Have you ever been on the verge of death when something wakes you up,
And suddenly you realize you've been living life with eyes wide shut---
Or been in a room all by yourself and you swear you hear a voice,
And it tells you not to give up yet...my friend you have a choice.
Have you ever been at the very bottom and then you take a look around,
And suddenly you realize that rock bottom is solid ground---
Or lost the one you loved the most, just gone without a trace,
But then you turn around and see him in a stranger's face.
Have you ever looked around and realized all your friends are bad,
And then you start to wonder where are all the good friends that you had---
Then as you start to wonder how this could have happened to your life,
You come across a book that tells you how to get it right---
You've seen this book before and you know that it can help,
But for some reason this book's place has always been up on your shelf---
Have you ever had the hardest time just standing on two feet,
Cause the only thing you've ever loved is buried six feet deep---
Or find yourself throughout each day just trying to remember
That day you told me you'd be okay that birthday in September.
Have you ever wondered what it is that puts these things in place,
The friends you meet, the dead-end street, the voice without a face.
I'll tell you what it is so you can stop wondering so much.
It's the miracles and the ups and downs from God's almighty touch.

So, when you're feeling down and like you can't make it on your own,
Just know that God is there for you to take his hand and lead you home.

Written by: Gigi

Reach for God

Written by: Gigi
September, 2018

My head is stuck up in the sky.
I'm reaching but I can't attain.
I spent my whole life asking why,
But now I only ask for pain.
I used to know what I believe
In my dreamer's state of mind.
Then reality took hold of me
With a life that's been unkind.
I close my eyes and scream for help
With violence in my tears.
I hope that God can hear my yell
With pain beyond my years.
I can't believe I'm still alive
When death is my best friend.
And the Devil and I have toed the line
From beginning to the end.
I like to think that it's made me strong
To go what I've gone through.
But is it wrong that I still long
For memories of you?
A tortured soul I reach for God
In whom I still believe.
I guess I know that through it all
He's never leaving me.
There's nothing left; I've cried it all.
The pain is never ending.
I guess what's left is to dry it all
With the love that you've been sending.

Loudest Silence

The loudest sound in a subtle world
Is the sound of silence, the sounds unheard.
The silent screams of a torn and shackled soul.
The loud silence of a happiness I've never known.
Truth be told, I'm broken behind my plastered smile.
What I've known has been dying all the while.
A monotonous cycle like on and off.
When I trust, I pay the cost.
Endless promises of love and loyalty
Come crashing down when depression gets a hold of me.
I guess I am unlovable because I am broken.
Actions speak louder than words unspoken.
How do I fight through a fog of confusion?
What do I do once death seems amusing?
Grab the noose and knot it tight,
Say my prayers, give up the fight.
Smiling faces making promises they cannot keep.
They always back away once things get deep.
I feel like I am drowning in an ocean full of regret.
In a pool of hope I swim but don't get wet.
Sometimes I wonder if anyone will ever care enough to see me
Or just always be forever grateful not to be me.
I can't hear myself over the noise inside my own mind...
The loudest place I've EVER been, an oxymoron of kind.
I act like I don't understand, but inside I know the truth...
I'll be forever haunted by the memories of my youth.

Written by: Gigi
February, 2018

Slaves No More

By: Mary Ray
2017 (For Daniel)

Here I lie on this cold concrete floor,
My heart's a black hole no feelings anymore.
The door will not open the locks clicked in place.
The guards walk the halls I'm stuck in this space.
How did this happen I truly can't say
The reason our lives have turned out this way.
Once we were happy our family in place
Now I have trouble remembering your face.
Our kids are now scattered like dust in the wind
Out of control our lives steady spin.
From one pill, to two, to ten it grew.
Used money for bills didn't know what to do.
First goes the house we'll live in our car.
Sleeping in the woods, stealing from stores.
Cooking on fires, fighting off bugs.
Not enough kisses not any hugs.
Stressing and fighting no money for pills.
No rehab will take us but this jail sure will.
We stole from our families, lost all our friends
So here we sit in River Bend.
We wait for the judge to seal our fates
In separate cells we must sit and wait.
We're here for a reason brought on by ourselves,
Sitting here in our personal hells.
We're now free from drugs our perspectives in place
We can have a good future but still we must wait.
The drugs of the past will not see our future.
We must fix our lives it's our only solution.

238

You are my soul mate, my heart, my strength
And our love will survive this that I guarantee.
So, I'll see you real soon when they unlock these doors
And we won't be slaves to drugs anymore.

Sisters Behind Bars

By: Mary Ray
2017

We sit here locked behind this razor wire wall,
Can't unlock the doors or walk down the halls.
The choices we've made have landed us here.
No love to be found, or family near.
We have no control the judge seals our fate.
All we can do now is sit here and wait.
Our charges are different from drugs, theft, and guns.
We can't see our daughters or hold our young sons.
This makes us a family, one Father we serve
Hoping for salvation we may not deserve.
But God says we're wrong to him we belong
And when in his grace we can pray for our wrongs.
We pray for each other us sisters in bars,
Cry for one another and try to stay strong.
God has a plan the bible has promised,
Our kids we'll have back and be happy mamas.
He's saving our lives that we've been living wrong
And we have his promise we will never be alone.

Forever Free

By: Mary Ray
August, 2017

I am somebody's mother, sister, and friend.
I have a husband who loves me and misses my hand.
I haven't seen my family in so many days,
Since I got myself locked up in this place.
I've met many women their stories like mine
Locked in with me doing our time.
We've become like a family just trying to survive.
While we're here just doing our time.
We've all felt depressed, down, and afraid
And many of us didn't know how to pray.
Then one Thursday morning they called us to church
And a group of strong ladies showed us our worth.
They took all the pain and shame we were feeling
And showed us that God tests us for a reason.
They gave us Bibles and showed us the steps
So that the Lord could give us some help.
They showed us love when they had no reason
And were always there to help those of us grieving.
Now when we get out our lives will be better.
We've found our salvation and friends we'll lose never.
So, we want to say Thank You for sharing your time
And helping us all to re-train our minds.
For now we'll be forever free
Thanks to all of you beautiful ladies.

Not Yet Well

By: Tanner

difficult to see
though eyes wide open
the path I've found
dark, lost, and hopeless
I'm not yet well
soon I hope to be
secrets I'll not tell
seems strange still to me
it is purpose I seek
it's hell that I've found
the wolves ready to eat
don't dare make a sound
a heart turned cold
a soul stained black
beginning to mold
beginning to crack
as fear settles in
confidence removed
feeling empty again
like nothing's been proved
continuing to stumble
I walk this dark path
striving to be humble
in wake of its wrath

Ups and Downs

Sometimes I'm up;
Sometimes I'm down.
Sometimes I smile;
Sometimes I frown.
Sometimes I laugh;
Sometimes I cry.
Sometimes I fall;
Sometimes I fly.
Sometimes I'm sure;
Sometimes I doubt.
Sometimes I'm nice;
Sometimes I pout.
Sometimes I'm strong;
Sometimes I'm weak.
Sometimes I'm proud;
Sometimes I'm meek.
No matter what
My mood may be,
One thing I know
Is God loves me!

* *

Psalm 143:8
*Let the morning bring me word of your unfailing
love, for I have put my trust in you. Show me the
way I should go, for to you I entrust my life.*

* *

When I Was A Child

Matthew 18:3
And he said: "Truly I tell you, unless you change and become like little children, you will never enter the kingdom of heaven."

Let Them Be Little

This section of the book is different from the rest. In my opinion, children are some of God's favorite people. As He said in **Mark 10:15,** *"Truly I tell you, anyone who will not receive the kingdom of God like a little child will never enter it."* We should strive every day to see our world through the eyes of children. We should never lose the wonder and excitement of this world that God created just for us.

The following poems are short and hopefully a little comical, and I hope that you will read them to your children. The years of childhood pass so swiftly that we often miss some of the best parts. I have tried to remember some of the little things that we might take for granted on a daily basis. **Psalm 127:3** reminds us that *"Children are a heritage from the LORD, offspring a reward from him."*

It is important that children be taught about God and salvation at an early age. The Bible has many verses concerning children. Most of us are probably familiar with **Proverbs 22:6** which states *"Start children off on the way they should go, and even when they are old they will not turn from it."* This world in which we reside has become so corrupt that our children and grandchildren must face temptations that we never could have dreamed would exist. Satan lures them any way he can, and only God can keep them safe.

Jesus Christ loved children and mentioned them often. He was quite explicit when He uttered the words in **Matthew 19:14…** *Jesus said, "Let the little children come to me, and do not hinder them, for the kingdom of heaven belongs to such as these."* How wonderful it is that we are all children of God!!! He is our Father, and we are heirs with Jesus Christ. We can take comfort in the truth of **Galatians 4:7** which states, *"So you are no longer a slave, but God's child; and since you are his child, God has made you also an heir."* May we always praise God with the fervor of children and worship Him with love and laughter!

Romans 8:28
And we know that in all things God works for
the good of those who love him, who have
been called according to his purpose.

The Spider Web

One lazy day as I sat still
Staring at my window sill,
I watched a spider working hard
Spinning her web yard-by-yard.

When she had finished her design,
She caught a bug fat and fine.
I asked, as I slapped at a gnat,
"Hey, do you want flies with that?"

* *

Ecclesiastes 5:19
*Moreover, when God gives any man wealth and possessions,
and enables him to enjoy them, to accept his lot and
be happy in his work---this is a gift of God.*

Colossians 3:23-24
*Whatever you do, work at it with all your
heart, as working for the Lord,
not for men, since you know that it is the Lord Christ you are serving.*

2 Thessalonians 3:10
*For even when we were with you, we gave you this rule:
"If a man will not work, he shall not eat."*

* *

Counting Sheep

I've tossed and turned; I cannot sleep.
My Daddy said, "Try counting sheep."
I thought he must have lost his mind.
We have no sheep that I can find.
He said to me, "Just close your eyes
And picture clear blue spacious skies.
Now see a field with grass so green
Covered with sheep---a lovely scene.
Then picture it as each one leaps
Over a fence with graceful sweeps.
Now as they jump just count each sheep,
And soon you will be fast asleep."
It worked a while, then I grew tense,
When one sheep got caught in that fence.

* *

Psalm 100:3
Know that the LORD is God.
It is he who made us, and we are his;
we are his people, the sheep of his pasture.

Psalm 119:176
I have strayed like a lost sheep.
Seek your servant,
for I have not forgotten your commands.

* *

Daisy Rose

Once in a village called Montrose
There lived a girl named Daisy rose.
As she strolled inside her garden,
A bee said, "I beg your pardon,
But you are treading in my space."
That bee then landed on her face.
From Daisy Rose a shriek arose
When that bee stung Rose on her nose.
That bee had such a perfect aim,
Her flowers never smelled the same.

* *

2 Corinthians 2:15
For we are to God the aroma of Christ among those who
are being saved and those who are perishing.

* *

Ford's Photo Fiasco

One day I was just being good,
Behaving like I thought I should.
I sat there counting all my toes;
Then Mom said I would have to pose.

I asked her, "Just what do you mean?"
I didn't want to cause a scene,
But I had no desire to be
Some model for the world to see.

I stood my ground and made a face.
My temper flared; my heart did race.
I told her, "No! I will not pose,
And don't you try to change my clothes!"

Well, as you see, my mommy won.
Before I had a chance to run,
My clothes were changed, and there I sat.
She even made me wear a hat!

A camera was in my face;
I wanted to escape this place!
They said to smile. I thought, "Yeah, right!"
I won't give up without a fight.

I knew I was smarter than they,
Because I ALWAYS get my may.
I came up with an evil plot,
For what they wanted, I DID NOT!

I threw the hat off of my head
And turned the other way instead.
I would not smile; I would not grin.
This battle I was sure to win.

I looked away from side-to-side.
I longed for somewhere I could hide.
"Stubborn" could be my middle name,
And I knew how to play this game!

Hey, look! I think they've had enough.
I guess I showed them who is tough!
I've shed some tears and thrown a fit,
And I've been mad enough to spit.

This photo session's over now,
So, I will smile and take a bow.
Though Mom and Nana are so cross,
I surely showed them who's the boss!

* *

James 3:17-18
But the wisdom that comes from heaven is first of all
pure; then peace-loving, considerate, submissive, full of
mercy and good fruit, impartial and sincere. Peacemakers
who sow in peace reap a harvest of righteousness.

* *

Homework

Homework! What a silly chore!
Finish some and then there's more.
Through my books for hours I pore.
Homework! It's an awful bore.

Homework! That's each teacher's rule,
Taking hours after school.
If I don't, I'll be a fool.
Homework! I think it's not cool.

* *

2Timothy 2:15
Study to show thyself approved unto God, a
workman that needeth not to be ashamed,
rightly dividing the word of truth. (KJV)

* *

King Kong

I went to see a movie
About the ape King Kong.
Then as they showed him to me,
I knew something was wrong.

It made no sense---none at all,
No, not one little bit.
That theater was so small,
How could that big ape fit?

* *

Mark 9:24
Immediately the boy's father exclaimed, "I do
believe; help me overcome my unbelief!"

* *

LEAD LINE

I sit tall in the saddle when I ride
With someone I trust walking by my side.
I smile and wave at my adoring fans,
And blow them kisses from my little hands.

I may be too young to talk or to read,
But I sure can handle my trusty steed;
And some older people---more than a few---
Just wish they could ride as well as I do!

I know why the judge can't seem to decide
When he sees how well each of us can ride.
We all get blue ribbons 'cause we're so fine.
It's great to be champions of our lead line!

* *

Psalm 147:10-11
*His pleasure is not in the strength of the horse, nor his
delight in the legs of the warrior; the LORD delights in those
who fear him, who put their hope in his unfailing love.*

* *

Merry-Go-Round

Up and down---I am riding high.
If I reach up, I'll touch the sky!
My pony's prancing round-and-round,
And music's playing some sweet sound.
As I go 'round, it makes me glad
Each time I spy my mom and dad.
It seems, no matter how I flee,
That other horse keeps catching me.
I'm riding hard to win this race;
I think by now I'm in first place.
As we stop at the finish line,
I'm thrilled to know that victory's mine!

* *

Psalm 147:10-11
His pleasure is not in the strength of the horse,
nor his delight in the legs of a man;
the LORD delights in those who fear him,
who put their hope in his unfailing love.

* *

Mud Pies

Mom's in her kitchen, and I am in mine.
We're preparing feasts on which we will dine.
My kitchen's outside beneath two big trees;
Air conditioning is a nice cool breeze.
While Mom cooks her meals in her pots and pans,
I make my cuisine in jars and tin cans.
I pour in some water, then add some dirt.
A few ground-up leaves surely could not hurt.
When the mixture's right, I pat out each pie
And place them on steps so they'll soon be dry.
But like other times---it often occurs---
I smell Mom's cooking. I think I'll eat hers.

✻ ✻

Romans 14:14
*As one who is in the Lord Jesus, I am fully convinced
that no food is unclean in itself. But if anyone regards
something as unclean, then for him it is unclean.*

✻ ✻

My Night Light

I do not need a night light in my little room
To chase away the shadows or dispel the gloom.
My mother thinks I may be afraid of the dark.
I don't fear my closet's a place where goblins park.
I don't think that monsters reside under my bed,
Or Freddy Krueger's waiting to slice off my head.
I'm not scared; I am brave. That's true without a doubt.
"Mom, come into my room! My night light just went out!"

* *

John 8:12
When Jesus spoke again to the people, he said, "I am
the light of the world. Whoever follows me will never
walk in darkness, but will have the light of life."

* *

Piggy Bank

I found a shiny penny
As I walked down the street.
I never find too many
Just lying at my feet.
I put it in my pocket
And took it home with pride.
I ran fast like a rocket
And carried it inside.
To me it was a treasure;
It made me feel so big.
It gave me so much pleasure
When I could feed my pig!

* *

Matthew 6:19-21
*Do not store up for yourselves treasures on earth, where moth
and rust destroy, and where thieves break in and steal. But store
up for yourselves treasures in heaven, where moth and rust
do not destroy, and where thieves do not break in and steal.
For where your treasure is, there your heart will be also.*

* *

Playing Dress-up

I'm all dressed up in Mommy's clothes,
In Mommy's shoes, and Mommy's hose.
I've fixed my hair and donned Mom's hat.
I ask myself, "Do I look fat?"
Now it is time to fix my face,
So I search through Mom's makeup case.
I paint my cheeks all nice and pink.
My lipstick should be red, I think.
My eye shadow should be bright blue.
Mascara's next. I'm nearly through.
Now I'm the fairest ever seen.
It's hard to be a beauty queen!

* *

Psalm 45:11
The king is enthralled by your beauty; honor him, for he is your lord.

* *

Shaving with Dad

Dad, stand me up right next to you
As we look in the mirror.
I like to do the things you do,
Dad, move a little nearer.
Now here we two stand side-by-side;
I see both our reflections.
This time within my heart I'll hide
Among my recollections.
We'll lather up and then begin
A new father-son routine.
When Mom sees us, I know she'll grin
With our faces shaved so clean.

* *

Psalm 127:3
Sons are a heritage from the Lord, children a reward from him.

* *

Sharing

No! I will not share my toy---
Not with a girl or a boy!
This is mine and mine alone.
You should get one of your own.
You might drop mine on the floor,
Then I would have mine no more.
You might wind it up too tight.
You might leave it on all night,
Then the battery would be
No more use to you or me.
Don't ask me, for goodness sake,
To share a toy you might break.
Of all the nerve! Wait! I see
Your new toy. Please share with me!

* *

1 Timothy 6:18
Command them to do good, to be rich in good deeds,
and to be generous and willing to share.

Hebrews 13:16
And do not forget to do good and to share with others,
for with such sacrifices God is pleased.

Luke 3:11
John answered, "The man with two tunics should share with him
who has none, and the one who has food should do the same."

* *

The Amusement Park

Amusement parks give me a thrill;
All through my bones I feel a chill.
They do not frighten me at all,
Although I am so very small.
On any ride I'll take your dare,
For I am brave; I do not scare.
I am willing and rough and tough!
Alas, I am not tall enough.

* *

I Corinthians 16:13
Be on your guard; stand firm in the faith,
be men of courage; be strong.

* *

The Doctor Visit

My doctor had a needle
At least twelve inches long.
So, I began to wheedle;
I said, "Wait! Something's wrong!
When you took your doctor's vow,
You swore you'd do no harm;
But that thing you're holding now
Is longer than my arm!"

* *

Matthew 9:12
On hearing this, Jesus said, "It is not the healthy
who need a doctor, but the sick."

* *

The Fall

When Jack and Jill
    went up that hill,
Why did Jack fall down
    and break his crown?
Did he get a shove
    from Jill above?
Had he made her mad
    or made her sad?
Did he push her first
    and act his worst?
Had he made her cry
    or made her sigh?
Were her feelings hurt,
    or did he flirt?
Did his feet just slip,
    or did he trip?
Did his knee give way
    and make him sway?
Was the sun too bright
    and obscured his sight?
Did he try to trot
    and get too hot?
Did he try to race
    to win first place?
Was the hill too steep
    or the well too deep?
When he took his spill,
    did he grab for Jill?
Did they ever mend?
    How'd the story end?
At the bottom of that hill,
what became of Jack and Jill?

* *

Psalm 37:23-24

If the LORD delights in a man's way, he makes his steps firm;
though he stumble, he will not fall, for the
LORD upholds him with his hand.

Psalm 55:22

Cast your cares on the LORD and he will sustain you;
he will never let the righteous fall.

* *

The Mud Puddle

One bright and clear sunshiny day
My mama sent me out to play.
As I began to run around,
A hole with mud is what I found.
I quickly looked about, and then,
I slowly put my right foot in.
The left foot followed close behind.
Soon my whole body was all "slimed."
Then something seemed to be amiss;
I never could explain all this.
Will Mom believe me when I say,
"That puddle just got in my way"?

* *

Matthew 26:41
"Watch and pray so that you will not fall into temptation.
The spirit is willing, but the body is weak."

* *

Vee Formation

I saw some geese go flying by
Way up high in the sky.
I imagined how it would be
Flying free in that vee.
What grand adventures could be found
Looking down at the ground.
I let my mind slowly release
To sweet peace with those geese.
I felt as if I had been freed.
They agreed I could lead.

* *

Isaiah 40:31
but those who hope in the LORD will renew their strength.
They will soar on wings like eagles; they will run and not grow weary,
they will walk and not be faint.

* *

Zoo Trip

A lion growled at me today;
I growled right back at him.
Some seals waved along my way;
I smiled and waved at them.
A monkey stared with beady eyes
And a ferocious frown.
That monkey did not realize
He could not stare ME down!
Some pink flamingos stood so still
While standing on one leg.
I thought it could cause quite a spill
If one should lay an egg.
A peacock chased me through the zoo
And tried to bite my heel.
I yelled, "Hey, peacock, I think you
Might make a tasty meal."
An elephant raised up his trunk,
And all could hear his gripes.
I saw a zebra and a skunk,
And they were both in stripes.
I saw giraffes with necks so long.
One place was filled with snakes.
I hope that glass is extra strong
And thick, for all our sakes!

* *

Genesis 6:19-20
*You are to bring into the ark two of all living creatures, male
and female, to keep them alive with you. Two of every kind of
bird, of every kind of animal and of every kind of creature that
moves along the ground will come to you to be kept alive.*

* *

Printed in the United States
By Bookmasters